The City and the Fields

Multicultural Themes in Modern California Literature

Marek Breiger

Valley Memories Press
Fremont, CA

Valley Memories Press
1401 Red Hawk Circle, Apt. 105
Building I
Fremont, CA 94538

ISBN: 978-0-9913652-0-3

Design and typesetting: Margaret Copeland, Terragrafix
Cover illustration: Dan Marlin
Publication Coordination: Naomi Rose
Proofreading: Gabriel Steinfeld

This book is for my mother, Florence Breiger, and in memory of my father, Boris Breiger (1927-2009), both of whom inspired me with their love of California history and literature. Thanks Mom for your constant faith, encouragement and support

The book is also for my brother, David, and my sister Mimi (1960-1982), for what we shared growing up in Stockton in the Great Central Valley, the San Joaquin.

Much thanks also to my companion Flo Leverenz for her patience and support during this many-year project.

Table of Contents

Preface

"What America is to the world," Robert Penn Warren once wrote, in reference to John Steinbeck, "California is to America." California literature reflects major themes of American literature in terms of the dreams of refuge for the oppressed, justice for the poor, dreams of new beginnings. California literature is multi-regional and multicultural, and its realism illustrates just how far we have come—and how far we need to go, in this volatile state of 38 million souls—to achieve true equality.

My grandparents were Jewish immigrants who settled in Chicago, who came to America in search of freedom. A generation later, their children and grandchildren came to California—as did so many of my classmates and parents—in search of a more democratic life. California was not only a place of physical beauty but also a place where white Oklahomans and Louisiana Blacks, Italian fishermen and Portuguese farmers and Chinese laborers, Sikh farmers and Mexican fieldworkers, elderly Russian Jews and Armenian refugees came in search of a better life. Yet we knew and know so little about each other, despite a powerful regional literature—as powerful as any in America.

I discovered Steinbeck and Saroyan in high school, and reading them gave me a place to stand. For both men were part of a specific California region and people. And both could see themselves in others. We were all, to quote my San Francisco State history professor Moses Rischin, "the children and grandchildren of immigrants and minority groups"; and that should unite us rather than divide us.

The City and the Fields is an examination of California literature from the beginning of the 20th century with Jack London, to the end of the 20th century with Amy Tan, and the beginning of the 21st century with Gerald Haslam.

My themes are both universal and multicultural—and still, I believe, current and foundational for all the new California writers who are working in the tradition of London, John Muir, John Steinbeck, and William Saroyan.

I believe that our important California writers should be read as part of California Literature classes in high school and college. Thus, this book is for students and teachers—and for fellow Californians who want to know more about those millions of souls who share our geography, remembering what Saroyan once said: "People are places." We cannot and should not separate landscape from humanity. Literature allows us to relate to others and "the other."

California literature allows us to understand how—from the First Peoples in California to the most recent immigrants—we are a part of something: a procession, hopefully (in Thomas Wolfe's words) "tending toward justice," that is larger than ourselves. Our writers confront injustice as a way to move us toward justice. California literature gives us hope. Yet a great literature should be read; and too many Californians, including those who love literature, know little about their own state and a literature that implicates us all.

Thus, themes related to the gulf between the economic classes are identified in essays dealing not only with London and Steinbeck but also with Tillie Olsen and the literary photographer Dorothea Lange, as well as Charles Bukowski and Horace McCoy. Sadly, the gulf of the rich and poor that they address still defines much of our state.

If Saroyan introduced the meaning of multiculturalism in California literature, the idea that he could be both proudly Armenian and Fresno-Californian-American, then other writers—notably Gary Soto, Richard Rodriguez, Amy Tan, and many more—followed suit in their own way. Latino writers such as Floyd Salas and Jose Villareal, for example, would later amplify and describe in their unique way how to display ethnic pride and at the same time be fully Californian, fully American.

Japanese-American writers, such as Saroyan's contemporary and friend Toshio Mori, are also featured in this book, along with the author of the powerful *17 Syllables*, Hisaye Yamamoto, and the most famous of all Japanese-American authors, Jean Wakatsuki Houston, author (with her husband James Houston) of *Farewell to Manzanar*.

Two powerful Chinese-American writers, Frank Chin and Maxine Hong Kingston, illustrate the diversity within each ethnic group—and show in their disagreements how important it is not to stereotype members of any group as being a carbon copy of one another.

The reality of mixed ethnicity is handled by Gerald Haslam, himself both Latino and Anglo. And our First Californians are featured in essays about Theodora Kroeber's *Ishi* as well as Malcolm Margolin's *The Ohlone Way.*

Gay rights—and the tension, as well as love, between gay adult children and their parents—are taken up in an essay about Dorothy Bryant's *A Day in San Francisco.*

California's environmental crisis is covered by John Muir and by Wallace Stegner, both featured in essays here.

The state of violence in California's big cities is the subject of an essay about modern-day Oakland by Jess Mowry—who, in many ways, updates Jack London's realistic view of an earlier Oakland—as well as Maya Angelou, who, like London, eventually found in Oakland and San Francisco more than the brutality of its mean streets.

I include, too, an essay on Joan Didion, and her realistic look at San Francisco and Los Angeles during a time of urban crisis in the 1960s, a time she does not romanticize but faces with great honesty.

In this book, I write about California authors who do more than offer polemics. Yet they do not shy away from the issues of the time: on the contrary, whether in fiction or nonfiction, these authors touch upon issues that are still relevant today:

- The meaning of ethnic identity and diversity
- Class as a controlling factor in many a Californian's life
- The debate over Affirmative Action
- The Bilingualism debate
- Racial stereotypes
- Environmental survival
- California as a promised land.

These issues have not been fully resolved in the years since 1989, when I began to publish essays about California writers—first as a guest essayist in *California English,* courtesy of the award-winning novelist, editor, essayist, and short-story writer Gerald Haslam.

California's best books are still classic, still contemporary. I feel strongly that these books could and would help us as Californians and Americans: that, after 9/11, we could learn from Manzanar and not make the mistake of internment; that Saroyan's description of Armenians in Fresno finding refuge from genocide would resonate with other refugees from genocide; that Luis Valdez' *La Bamba* would give present-day ethnic Californians an insight into the difficulty as well as possibilities of having more than one identity.

My belief as a teacher and writer is that our powerful California literature—as powerful as any regional American literature—allows us to become a link from the past to the future. My belief is that we can share an identity that is geographic but also transcends places on a map—an identity based on a true appreciation of a writer like Steinbeck as well as others, writers whose books are great enough to become a plea for justice and compassion that unites us all.

The essays included in *The City and the Fields* have appeared in: *California English*; the anthology, *Updating the Literary West* (Texas Christian University); *Western American Literature*; *Inside English*; *San Francisco Chronicle*; *Redwood Coast Review*; and the anthology, *To Honor a Teacher* (Andrew McMeel, editor). Three of the essays in this book appear for the first time. My thanks to former editor of *California English*, Wanda Burzycki, and to the present editor, Carol Jago, both of whom allowed me the freedom to write about my vision of California literature without imposing any guidelines on my freedom of expression. And a special thanks to Gerald Haslam, who gave me a chance to be a guest columnist and then a columnist in *California English*.

Thanks also to my friend, Sam Hardin (1923-2012), whose knowledge of California literature helped me to see the depth of "unknown writers" like Jose Villareal and Hisaye Yamamoto.

And my salute, too, to all the important and powerful California writers who do not appear in this book.

— *Marek Breiger, July 2013*
Fremont, California

PART I
Background

(from top left, clockwise) Ishi, Jack London, cover of Sam Fow: The San Joaquin Chinese Legacy *by Sylvia Sun Minnick (with permission from Sylvia Sun Minnick)*

CHAPTER I

From Rebellion to Reconciliation

Jack London to Amy Tan

The twentieth century has closed in as barbaric a way as it began. The murder of children, now commonplace; poverty amidst wealth; the savagery of business downsizing; racial division, exacerbated by haters of all colors: all define us now, in California as in the nation.

Jack London

Jack London was California's first great twentieth-century writer. Frank Norris, our major novelist of the nineteenth century, who would die in 1902 at the age of 32, predicted that the American literature of the new century would lead us into "a world of the workingman, crude of speech, swift of action, strong of passion, straight to the heart of a new life." London would personify Norris's prophecy. He would take California and American literature into the streets and Alaskan wilderness, into the saloons and canneries and waterfront bars.

London would preach socialism and the hope of human progress, but he would not have been surprised by our lack of progress as we end the century he began. He knew the base as well the noble instincts within humankind and within himself.

In January 1900, he turned 24 years old, and already he had led a life as full as men twice his age. Born illegitimate and in poverty, he had been an Alaskan gold miner, a seasoned drinker, an oyster pirate, a fighter, a sailor who had seen the great ports of the world, a "road kid" who had been with Coxey's Army during the March on Washington of 1894. He had spent time in prison; he was a boy of the Oakland streets and waterfront, self-made and self-educated, a writer who would brave, if necessary, a thousand rejection slips to rise to the heights of California and American life and literature.

He was a California rebel and dreamer, caught between two ways of life. London had strong instincts for life and a strong desire to efface life's suffering through embracing death. He represents, still, all of those who defy the stifling expectation of family, society, and peers. London exemplified the rebel instinct that turns violence into art, which out of self seeks more than self. London found a tragic truth. But he found more than tragedy.

Both his love of life and his desire for death are found in one of London's strongest works, a book that is still contemporary, the deceptively named autobiography *John Barleycorn*. Published in 1913, just three years before his death, *John Barleycorn* is all about and yet more than about London's battle with alcohol. It illustrates London's perception of life as a painful illusion. Alcohol confirmed London's darkest intuitions about the futility of all life.

Yet the autobiography, as does all of London's writing, shows the rewards of a life lived heroically. London is still revered because, despite his disillusion, he celebrated courage, love, sacrifice, and valor. He honored the courage he found in others as well as himself. In bad times, London showed heroic effort. His theme, whether in "A Piece of Steak," "To Build a Fire," *Valley of the Moon*, *The Road*, *Martin Eden*, or *John Barleycorn*, relates to the inevitability of loss. We cannot overcome, thought London, either the power of nature or the power of human malevolence. But we can, he makes clear, make our fight with dignity and courage. We have an obligation to face life with our best effort, to live in a way not degrading to ourselves or to others. London's hope for a better California, whether through socialism or through a reclamation of land, was individual. He expected others to show some of the bravery that he had shown. London's life, as reflected in his writing, has meaning for us in California today.

London was filled with contradictions and flaws. He was courageous yet alcoholic, man of the revolution yet racially prejudiced, lover of family yet deserter of family, celebrator of life and celebrator of death. His story can be found in his short fiction and long fiction, in essays and reportage. From *The Call of the Wild* to *The People of the Abyss*, London made his mark as a world writer. But it is *John Barleycorn* that gives us as clear a picture as we have of the beginning of our modern California time. London is the prose poet of our cities and countryside as the century turned, one hundred years ago, in California.

The Autobiography Itself

Perhaps London should have stuck with his original title for *John Barleycorn—Sailor on Horseback*, the title that would be used later, with much success, by London's biographer Irving Stone. For *John Barleycorn* is no more about drinking per se than Claude Brown's *Manchild in the Promised Land* is only about gangs, or *The Autobiography of Malcolm X* is only about religion. London's attempt to understand and come to terms with his drinking moved him toward truths about himself and his companions and to universal truths about human strivings, compromises, and loss.

In *John Barleycorn*, London defines Oakland, California, as it was in the 1890s and the first decade of the twentieth century, with its street brutality, its divisions based on class, its cruel exploitation of adult and child labor.

For London, everything is person. Of his factory work, he would write that he did not know of a horse in the city of Oakland who worked the hours he worked or suffered the treatment he suffered. London's understanding rings all too true today. From *John Barleycorn*:

> ...I saw the wheels of the social machine go around, and I learned that the dignity of manual labor wasn't what I had been told it was by the teachers, preachers, and politicians. The men without trades were hopeless cattle...I couldn't see any dignity at all. And when a workman got old, or had an accident, he was thrown into the scrapheap like any worn-out machine. I saw too many of the sort who were making anything but dignified ends of life....

Alcohol was intrinsic to London's life and time. He was honest and perceptive in his insights about drinking. He shows us the ways that drinking was both cause and effect of a brutal era. London was appalled at the devastation caused by drinking, yet he understood the appeal of alcohol as found in the communal spirit and camaraderie he had experienced in the working men's saloons of his youth and manhood. Though London voted in 1912 to ban alcohol, *John Barleycorn* is not an apology. The book defines the tension, illustrated by a life of heavy drinking, between a man's ideal of life and his life as it was actually lived.

And within the limits of his life, London demonstrated unusual bravery. He was a man who fought social injustice through words. In *Martin Eden*, London's autobiographical novel, the author makes explicit his disgust with turn-of-the-century labor conditions. From the novel:

> They have forced to worse horror than chattel slavery your slave boys and girls. Two million of your children are toiling today in this trader oligarchy of the United States. Ten millions of you slaves are not properly sheltered nor properly fed....

Yet London did not use social evil to justify his own behavior. He did not resort to criminality. (His brief prison stay was for a trumped-up vagrancy charge when he was with Coxey's Army.) London differs from the prison writers of our own time. London, knowing firsthand the horrors of society, did not endorse violence against the innocent; he battled injustice with words. *John Barleycorn* is the story of a man who struggles against his fate, who works impossible hours, who returns to school, who succeeds as a writer, who fights with his pen.

As I write, I think of those right-wing spokesmen who show no sympathy for the deprived, hurt, handicapped, or those unlike themselves. And I think, too, of some of my contemporaries: once 1960s radicals of the left who now remain silent about injustice from "our side"—including murder—so long as it is their lives and their jobs that are protected.

I think of London's strength and anger and honesty. Jack London was a man who was always himself. In these increasingly totalitarian

The City and the Fields

times, we could learn from London. He represented a multitude because he was true to himself. London exemplifies the beginning of modern California literature—personal, angry with injustice, individual in style yet universal in implication. The story of *John Barleycorn* is tragically applicable to California today.

Amy Tan and *The Joy Luck Club*

Amy Tan is to the ending of 20th-century California literature what Jack London was to its beginning. She has become the translator of common experience. In an age when everything seems broken, she defines the possibility of repair and reconciliation. In *The Joy Luck Club*, she writes not only for women or for Chinese or for Asian-Americans; she writes for all of us who struggle to find connection and value in our past.

She achieves her effects without sentimentality, for she understands that the past can cripple as well as free. *The Joy Luck Club* is not a paean to the life of World War II or pre-World War II China. The novel is an acknowledgment and a paying of respect for the suffering and basic humanity of the immigrant generation of Chinese women who have been so stereotyped by American society and so initially misunderstood by their own children.

Tan is a California writer, and like London before her, she is now a nationally and internationally acclaimed writer. The novel gains strength through specifically rendered settings in Oakland and San Francisco. From Tan's descriptions, the reader can imagine the vitality of San Francisco's Chinatown, the largest Chinatown in America, as it was during the 1950s, with its mix of generations, dialects, and tragic experiences.

Tan is a shrewd social critic and she exposes the vacuity of popular California culture that has run within the past twenty-five years the spectrum of shallowness and pretension, from hippie to yuppie. She moves us toward embracing a more painful, more real, more responsible way of life. Her book argues for the older values of obligation for—and responsibility toward—our family elders. In the context of our time, the speech of Lindo Jong seems not merely angry but an appropriate corrective:

I once sacrificed my life to keep my parents' promise. This means nothing to you, because to you promises mean nothing. A daughter can promise to come to dinner, but if she has a headache, if she has a traffic jam, if she wants to watch a favorite movie...she no longer has a promise.

Unlike many readers, I saw the film of *The Joy Luck Club* before reading the novel. In the theater, all around us, people wept as we viewed the heartfelt and touching conclusion. Our tears were not bitter. They were cathartic, for Tan has touched us honestly and deeply. We crave connection with our family and heritage. We desire an American culture that combines the best of our ancestry and America. But we have been left with a shallow, popular national culture, absorbed with morbidity and obsessed with violence; we are ignorant, most of us, of the strengths of our parents' and grandparents' world. Tan offers us something rare, a chance for reconciliation and hope. She destroys vicious stereotypes, but she does more than combat prejudice. When June finds the twin sisters that her late mother had suffered to protect but, despite her best efforts, had given up for dead, June has recovered her best self through understanding her mother's courage and best intentions. When June understands her mother's desperate life during the Japanese occupation of China, we understand the bonds of love that one generation has struggled to pass to another. A mother's spirit has been recovered:

> ...And I know it's not my mother, yet it is the same look she had when I was five and disappeared all afternoon, for such a long time, that she was convinced I was dead. And when I miraculously appeared, sleepy eyed, crawling from underneath my bed, she wept and laughed, biting the back of her hand to make sure it was true.
>
> And now I see her again, two of her, waving, and in one hand there is a photo, the Polaroid I sent them. As soon

The City and the Fields

as I get beyond the gate, we run toward each other, all three of us embracing, all hesitations and expectations forgotten.

"Mama, Mama," we all murmur as if she is among us....

Amy Tan's example defines a deep approach to multiculturalism in literature. We are moved by *The Joy Luck Club* not only because of the novel's ethnicity, though the novel's Chinese base is, of course, intrinsic. We are touched because of the human situations that Tan narrates and describes. We cannot feel sympathy for characters only because of their race or gender. We can feel empathy for characters whose struggle evokes our common human condition. For that reason, millions of the children and grandchildren of European immigrants revere and respect and are grateful to Amy Tan. Her success can be an example and a model for future writers of our state and our country-boys and -girls of all races and ethnicities. *The Joy Luck Club* is a human triumph.

Appealing to the "Better Angels"

"...Time and again successful stands were made by the firefighters, and every time the flames flanked around on either side or came up from the rear, and turned to defeat the hard-won victory.

"An enumeration of the buildings destroyed would be a directory of San Francisco.... An enumeration of the deeds of heroism would stock a library and bankrupt the Carnegie medal fund. An enumeration of the dead— will never be made...."

—*Jack London, "An Eyewitness's View of the San Francisco Earthquake"*

Between Jack London and Amy Tan stand a host of powerful 20th-century California writers, authors who have enumerated, with London, deeds of heroism and acts of redemption. Let me name some of them:

John Steinbeck • William Saroyan • Gerald Haslam • Luis Valdez • Ernesto Galarza • Jose Villareal • Wanda Coleman • Joan Didion • Ed Bullins • Arnold Rojas • Richard Dokey • Ella Leffland • Tillie Olsen • Hisaye Yamamoto • Jade Snow Wong • Maya Angelou • Maxine Hong Kingston • Gus Lee • Theodora Kroeber • Toshio Mori • Carey McWilliams • Joseph Wambaugh • Leonard Gardner • Malcolm Margolin • Dorothy Bryant • Wallace Stegner • Jean Wakatsuki Houston • James Houston • Gary Soto • Richard Rodriguez • Luis Rodriguez • Sylvia Sun Minnick • John Fante • Lawrence Powell • Floyd Salas • Wright Morris • Merle Haggard • and Elizabeth McDaniel.

There are many more. Our story, in these past more than a hundred years, has been painted in words.

We are not a race, but we can be a culture. Our California writers call for readers. It would be an act of sanity and survival to reclaim, through literature, our history. We need to realize that we share, in our state, human as well as physical geography. Our literature offers the clarity of universal understandings. Our writing can help us enter the new century with a deeper connection to the millions who share our place. California literature transcends racial, ethnic, class, and gender lines. But a great literature unread and unsung cannot help us.

As of now, we seem to celebrate our differences. All around us, fanatics of the right and of the left seek to impose their ideology upon literature and life. Our writers offer us something better. Between Jack London—with his rebellion against injustice and his citations of courage—and Amy Tan, with her stories of reconciliation, stand many writers that help us heal and remember, writers who offer recognitions that appeal to what Lincoln once called "the better angels of our nature." We approach the new century with a body of writing that can offer coming generations in California, and the nation, real catharsis, real laughter, real tears, and real hope.

CHAPTER 2

Native California History as Literature

Theodora Kroeber's *Ishi* and
Malcolm Margolin's *The Ohlone Way*

Perhaps only those who have suffered mass murder, apartheid, "ethnic cleansing," segregation, or pogrom can appreciate fully the misery of what first Spain, then Mexico, and finally the United States visited upon the indigenous people of California. Here, in California, before the Spanish arrival, lived more than 300,000 Indians, divided into 21 known nationalities or small nations. By 1910, the number of native Californians would be under 20,000.

The Spanish, despite the intentions of the more humane priests, initiated a mission system backed by invading Spanish soldiers that, writes ethnohistorian Edward Castillo (*The Californians*, Volume 10, Number 2), "...resembled nothing so much as the Caribbean plantation...." Castillo quotes an eyewitness, English sea captain Frederick Beechey, in an illustration of how religious belief became perverted into oppression and cruelty. Here is Beechey's account of a mass at Mission San Francisco in 1826:

> The congregation was arranged on both sides of the building, separated by a wide aisle along the center, in which were separated several bailiffs with whips, canes, and goads, to preserve silence and maintain order, and what seemed more difficult than either, to keep the congregation in their kneeling posture. The goads were better adapted to this purpose than the whip, as they would reach a long way, and inflict a sharp puncture

without making any noise. The end of the church was occupied by a guard of soldiers under arms with fixed bayonets....

Castillo records, as have other historians, testimony after testimony documenting the evils of the mission system. The Spanish system was cruel even in the context of a cruel time. Castillo quotes another observer, the French Catholic La Perouse, who wrote, "...Corporal punishment is inflicted on the Indians of both sexes who neglect the exercises of piety, and many sins which in Europe are left to divine justice are here punished by irons and stocks."

The Mexican rule of California, now much romanticized, was far from utopian. The Mexican ranchos were bound by caste and color, which, according to Gerald Haslam in *Many Californias*, "relegated those with Indian blood to subservient status." "The Indians," wrote James J. Rawls, cited by Haslam, "received nothing more than shelter, food, and clothing." Barbarism reached its height with the Anglo invasion. Beginning with the time of the Gold Rush, white Americans visited massacre and genocide against the California Indians.

Two historian anthropologists, Malcolm Margolin and Theodora Kroeber, have elevated narrative history to literary art. They have recreated a world, more than 3,000 years old, that was destroyed forever, beginning with the Spanish occupation. Their books—Margolin's *The Ohlone Way* and Kroeber's *Ishi*—have lessons for us in contemporary California. Through an understanding of the strengths of Ohlone and Ishi's Yahi culture, we might learn to live in harmony with both present-day California's natural environment and human cultures. Margolin and Kroeber detail Native Californian lives that were, in many ways, more humane than our own.

The Ohlone Way

Malcolm Margolin describes in *The Ohlone Way* the lives of these Native Americans on a typical year cycle before the Spanish came to California. The Ohlone name is used by Margolin to refer to the "40 or so independent tribelets found between Point Sur and the San Francisco Bay," whose people "spoke languages that had a common root and (to us) their customs appear broadly similar...."

Malcolm Margolin begins with a physical description of an unspoiled land; the Bay Area enjoyed the richest wildlife in North America:

> The channels were alive with beavers and river otters in fresh water, sea otters in salt water. And everywhere there were thousands and thousands of herons, curlews, sandpipers, dowitches, and other shore birds.... The geese that wintered in the Bay Area were "uncountable" according to Father Juan Crespi....
>
> "Animals seem to have lost their fear and become familiar with man," [wrote] Captain Beechey.

Margolin describes a time and a place where the hunter showed respect for the animals he knew he must kill. The Ohlone hunter showed reverence—not guilt—after a successful hunt, for he took only what was necessary. After killing a deer, for example, the hunter himself would eat little, reflecting on the soul of the animal he had taken.

Other of the Ohlone ways are not ones a modern could easily live with or accept. For all the nobility of the Ohlone religion, it sanctioned what is superstitious and primitive, and worse: "...A deformed baby or twin is full of malignant powers and killed...." It is to Margolin's credit that he does not attempt to justify or qualify this practice.

Other Ohlone practices—including incest taboos, which made necessary marriages outside the tribelet—were specific in helping the Ohlones in their intent to live in harmony with the world of nature. The Ohlone culture was a protective one, and within their play, games, and marriages, a love of children, a tolerance for others, and a respect for neighboring tribes was clearly expressed.

Children, especially, were valued, and here the Ohlone community had advanced far beyond the European practices of the time:

...During those early years parents, grandparents, and relations...watched over the children. The Ohlones were not strict parents; they did not whip or otherwise punish their children nor did they scold or shame them in public....

Margolin makes no attempt to present the Ohlone way as a model of, in his words, an "ideal society." He has, though, crucially understood that the Ohlone "...can provide us with a vision—a vision of how a Stone-Age people, a people whom we have so belittled, had in fact sustained a life of great beauty and wisdom...."

Margolin's last chapters are tragic in their details of a people humbled by the treatment of Spanish, Mexican, and Anglo California. Particularly sad, to Margolin, is the Mission system, a system viewed by Margolin as the invention not of depraved men but of "failed idealists" who, in their zeal to bring Christianity to the native Californian, brought "...not only physical death but spiritual death as well."

Margolin tells us that the Ohlone people had so much respect for their dead that they could not say the names of the departed; it was considered a blasphemy to speak the dead one's name.

We who have come after the Ohlone have shown our lack of respect for the Ohlone people in a different manner. We have not fully acknowledged their existence. We should recognize the Ohlone and mourn their passing. For we live where they once fished, hunted, gambled, prayed, told stories, made love, gave birth, laughed. We live in a place where a people had their laughter, their culture, their lives stolen from them. As Herbert Howe Bancroft wrote:

> ...The part of the early intercourse between aboriginal Americans and Europeans which properly belongs to history may be briefly given. The miners and settlers were arrogant and impatient; there were no missionaries or others present with even the poor pretext of soul saving or colonizing. It was one of the last human hunts of civilization.

Theodora Kroeber, in her classic *Ishi*, has given us a portrait of the people, the Yahi, and an individual, Ishi, called by his friend Professor Waterman, with some justice, "one of the great men of the century."

Ishi was a Yahi, a tribelet of the Yana nation, a people who had lived in the foothills of Mt. Lassen for more than 3000 years. Kroeber describes not the "Digger" Indian, a false myth, but an ancient people who lived, as did all the California Indians (the most populous group of Native Americans in North America), in a condition resembling that of Greek city-states.

The Yana and the Yahi organized their lives, as did the Ohlone, around harvest and fishing, hunting and storytelling. Children were prized and loved, and in the fierce northern climate an ancient people would, as described by Theodora Kroeber, listen in winter to the "retelling of old history of how animals and men were made... (and so with) the snow moon bringing a lightfall...the Yana cycle of changing seasons completed another full term...."

The Yana would avoid, because of location, the Spanish and Mexican regimes in California, but it would be their bad luck that in 1844 the Mexican government gave land grants bordering Yana territory so that "...in due course the United States government confirmed these grants...." If reading about Spanish and Mexican treatment of native Californians leaves one with anger, reading about the Anglo-Indian treatment of the California Indians is truly sickening. American treatment evokes images of the Nazi mass murder of Jewish communities, of KKK lynchings of Blacks, of Turkish genocide against the Armenians.

Kroeber describes the mass killings of the Yahi, in particular the butchery of two "Indian fighters"—Hi Good and R. A. Anderson, men who stopped at nothing in their bestiality. Eyewitness Sim Moak, quoted by Kroeber, has written:

> ...When a party of us settlers would start to clean
> up the Indians we would elect a captain and it would
> always be Good or Anderson. The captain was entitled
> to the scalps. At one time Good had forty hanging in
> the poplar tree by his house....

Theodora Kroeber reports acts of pure sadism:

> There was one young Yana woman, unusually popular with the white people who knew and employed her, who was dragged by force out of the white man's home where she lived. Her old aunt and uncle were taken and the three pumped full of bullets on the spot.... The man who killed her, and who was like "likkered up," was not satisfied. "I don't think that little squaw is dead yet," he is reported as saying. To make sure, he smashed in her skull with his revolver.

> The record piles up—an Indian woman and her baby killed here, three women at another place, twenty Yana of both sexes in the settlement of Cottonwood, and three hundred who were attending an autumn harvest festival at the head of Oak Run. Curtin's informant estimated the surviving to be about fifty persons.

Yahi response was discriminating. The Indians did not take retribution against all whites, but only upon those responsible for their own suffering. In a letter to Professor Waterman, Richard Gernon stated, "...It is a remarkable thing, that the white men who hunted the Mill Creek Indians, between the years 1853 and 1865, have always had their camps robbed in after years. And those who never hunted those Indians never had anything stolen from them by Indians...."

By 1911, the time of Ishi's discovery, the genocide was nearly complete and of all the Yahi, a lone man, Ishi, survived. After his discovery, Ishi, shivering, afraid, near to starving, was placed under protection in jail, where he refused food and water and seemed utterly in a state of mourning and loss.

What makes Kroeber's book more than a tragic documentary is her description of the last years of Ishi's life: that time, beginning in jail, when Ishi would meet one of the three men who would become his close friends. These three men—Professor Waterman; Alfred Kroeber (the author's husband); and Dr. Pope—would be invaluable in helping Theodora Kroeber describe not a relic or a symbol, but a living human being.

In jail, Professor Waterman, attempting to communicate with Ishi, breaks through with a Yahi word; and Ishi begins to regain his feeling.

> Ishi ventured to ask Waterman in Yahi, "Are you an Indian?" Waterman answered back that he was. The hunted look left Ishi's eyes…. Here was a friend. He knew…that Waterman was not an Indian.

Ishi was taken to U.C. Berkeley, where he voluntarily lived in a room at the museum and where he was employed explaining the culture of his people. Victimized by whites, Ishi did not hate. In an alien culture, Ishi retained his own culture. Waterman, Alfred Kroeber, and Dr. Pope describe a man of total dignity, complete honesty, capable of emotion and friendship—a man who would be unusual in any time or place.

With anthropologists Alfred Kroeber and Waterman, Ishi patiently instructed and explained Yahi ways and language. He joked with Dr. Pope and the interns at the hospital, but at the same time was asked by Dr. Pope to attend operations and to speak about Yahi ways of healing. Ishi was a man of faith who "…believed in a Land of the Dead where the souls of the Yana live out their community existence." Although he did not accept a new religion, "Christian doctrine interested him and seemed to be for the most part reasonable…." Perhaps 50 years old in 1912, he was an excellent athlete. Kroeber portrays a man, not a grown child: Ishi means "man" in Yahi. He would never disclose to his friends his Indian name. But he did tell his friends, on a trip with them back to his former home, about his concealment, about the customs and beliefs and stories of his people. He trusted his white friends with his story. Kroeber owes the strength of her book not only to her immense talent as a writer, but also to Ishi himself, who was willing to share his sorrows with the men whom he had learned to trust. The invaders of his land never gave to his people what Ishi has given to us.

Upon Ishi's death, Dr. Pope wrote, in eulogy:

He looked upon us as sophisticated children—smart but not wise. We knew many things, and much that is false. He knew nature, which is always true. His were the qualities of character that last forever. He was kind; he had courage and though all had been taken from him, there was no bitterness in his heart....

Final Thoughts

Reading *The Ohlone Way* and *Ishi* should give pause to our "native sons and daughters" as well as other Californians who use their years in our state as a weapon with which to put down more recent arrivals. In the context of Native California history, we are all recent immigrants. We are living on a land once inhabited by other people. We, who teach California literature, have a chance, I believe, to help create a more tolerant culture. We can teach books that acknowledge past suffering and honor the contributions of the many cultures that make up California. We can begin by teaching works like *Ishi* and *The Ohlone Way*, detailing the lives of the original inhabitants of our state, who, long before our arrival, lived here in caring communities, in harmony with nature, with respect for other living beings.

CHAPTER 3

Chinese Voices

Sylvia Sun Minnick

"I wrote this book to capture the total Chinese experience in one California county and in a community that became a city representative of all California's people."

—*Sylvia Sun Minnick*

Asian Californians are creating a major ethnic literature while contributing to the uniqueness and strength of California writing.

It did not begin with Amy Tan and Maxine Hong Kingston.

In the 1940s, literary pioneers like Toshio Mori, Hisaye Yamamoto, and Jade Snow Wong wrote their way into mainstream American and California literature while at the same time being true to their Asian-American experience. By now a wealth of Chinese, Japanese, and other Asian-American authors are available in anthologies such as *The Big Aiieee* and writers like Amy Tan and Maxine Hong Kingston are national voices.

Most Asian American writers have worked in the genres of the poem, play, short story, novel, and autobiography. Now Chinese California has produced a major historian. What Oscar Handlin, in *The Uprooted*, did for the European immigrants of Boston and the East Coast, what Gay Talese, in *All My Sons*, does for the Italian-American experience, what Irving Howe did for Eastern European Jewish immigrant life in *World of our Fathers*, Sylvia Sun Minnick achieves for the Chinese of California in *Sam Fow* (Panorama West Publishing, Fresno, California, introduction by Thomas Chinn).

Her book has a particular application to the research projects often done in junior year in California high schools in conjunction with

American Literature and U.S. History. Sun Minnick's narrative history of the Chinese of Stockton and San Joaquin County allows us to see the forces that created the elders, the children and grandchildren of present Chinese-Californians. Further, her explication of anti-Chinese racism is relevant to the prejudices against Asian-Americans that still persist.

Sam Fow

The discovery of gold was the impetus not only for white migration to California, but for Chinese as well. The Chinese who arrived in San Joaquin County came from the 24 districts of Guangdong Province, from three major and distinct dialect groups. Sun Minnick writes of the reasons for Chinese emigration, reasons that echo the experience of European immigrants.

> Emigration seemed the only solution to many problems in South China. In the mid-19th century China, and more particularly Guangdong Province, suffered not only from a series of natural and social disasters, but from the oppression of a decaying social system as well...

Thousands of Chinese sailed to California, clustering in three major cities here, all key to the Gold Rush: San Francisco, Sacramento, and Stockton. San Francisco was called "First City," the big city and home to America's largest Chinatown. One then made way by boat through the Golden Gate and Carquinez Straits to either the Sacramento or the San Joaquin River, disembarking at "Second City"—Sacramento, the center and jumping-off place for the northern mines—or Stockton. Sun Minnick writes:

> To the Chinese, Stockton was Sam Fow, third city, indicating it was the third stop on the way to the mines. There were many reasons Chinese gold seekers might travel to Stockton: the southern mines were rich, steerage fee was low, the voyage was relatively short.

And, initially, reaction to the Chinese was favorable.

> The editors of the *San Joaquin Republican* wrote, "The Chinaboys are amongst our best citizens. They are generally honest and industrious and very seldom figure in a police report. Such men are always welcome..."

Minnick places the early Chinese community within a multi-ethnic context; Chinatown grew between "two other immigrant communities," the Jewish and the German. Further, Chinatown was not originally a ghetto: "It should be noted that this Channel Street Chinese quarter was not an isolated settlement; the neighborhood was actually a co-mingling of different nationalities..."

Prejudice

Charles Weber, Stockton's founder, was not a man of prejudice, and his welcoming of persecuted peoples, including Chinese and Jews, as well as his friendship for Mexican-Californians, was unusual for an Anglo-Californian of his historical time. Yet, in San Joaquin County, the prejudice became fierce, ghettoization became practice, and Chinese contributions were ignored.

As in the rest of California, the Chinese contributions were invaluable to Stockton and San Joaquin County. In a superb chapter, "White Man's Vision, Chinese Labor," Sun Minnick details how Chinese sweat built the railroads, reclaimed the swamplands, and made the levees—levees that protect the Delta islands from flooding. For near slave labor pay, Chinese physical labor helped create the bounty of the great valley. Minnick writes: "It should be remembered that the Chinese provided the manpower when the Delta swamplands were first reclaimed."

The Chinese were a patient but not a passive people, and it is a mistake to believe that the Chinese did not understand the nature of their exploitation. The Chinese were cooperative, not given to random violence, but they were quite capable of standing up for their rights.

When Chinese were promised work but not hired, in one incident, "…the disappointed Chinese threw the foreman into the river and drove the white superintendent, Gen. T.H. Williams, and his staff off the island…" Though the Chinese ringleaders were identified and jailed, it is evident that the Chinese were quite aware of injustices meted out to them.

By the 1870s, anti-Chinese racism was evident. Hypocrisy was rampant and included all areas of Stockton and California society. As the Southern white aristocracy employed Blacks as trusted housekeepers while maintaining segregation, California's aristocracy did the same, entrusting to the Chinese the care of their households and children, while at the same time supporting laws for their exclusion and segregation.

More disheartening, the labor and feminist movements, instead of looking to build bridges toward the Chinese, spread hatred. It is ironic that the more cosmopolitan cities of San Francisco and Los Angeles, not "provincial" Stockton, were the centers of anti-Chinese prejudice.

> …10,000 gathered in San Francisco on July 23, 1877, to hear speeches on the eight hour day and nationalization of railroads. Speakers at this meeting incited the masses to riot against the San Francisco Chinese and after three nights of turbulence 25 Chinese laundries had been destroyed and an estimated $1 million of damage had occurred throughout the city.

In Los Angeles, in 1871, the violence was worse. To quote historian Kevin Starr (in *Inventing the Dream*) on the infamous L.A. riots of over 120 years ago: "…Before the day was over, seven Chinese males, including a boy of fourteen, died horrible deaths, tortured by the mob in the open street before being lynched…." What happened in Los Angeles can only be described as an American *pogrom*.

Reading about the nature of anti-Chinese sentiment should give pause to those who speak of historic America as if women and people of color had always been historically allied. For 19th-century California radicals and feminists, far from accepting the Chinese, scorned them. And California's Blacks, sadly, instead of viewing the Chinese as a fellow oppressed group, practiced prejudice against them.

It was Laura De Force Gordon, to quote Minnick,

> a lawyer, ardent suffragist, and one of the first women admitted to the California bar...who spearheaded the anti-Chinese political movement in San Joaquin County in 1885-1886.... For nearly an hour Mrs. Gordon told of the need for ridding California of its "hordes of Chinese filth and crime-breeding coolies."

Stockton's Chinese, denied access to white schools, enrolled their children in a "colored" school, only to face rejection and hatred. Ms. Minnick quotes a Stockton journalist of the time: "...as the colored have suffered enough from prejudice, unfortunately yesterday, they inflicted what they have felt...."

Minnick, wisely, refrains from editorializing. She narrates rather than argues. But the reader, on the basis of the facts, is confronted with an industrious, self-respecting people, who were treated with intolerance, prejudice, and, at times, expulsion and murder.

A Human Community

Minnick does not draw a community of saints. Early Chinatown was heavily populated by single men and these men had a huge burden. They were expected to send money and help care for their families in impoverished South China while they, themselves, were struggling for existence. With almost no women available as wives, prostitution in Chinatown was endemic and opium (legal until 1909) dispensed. Minnick describes, too, the brutal and bloody Tong wars of the 1920s.

Yet, under difficult conditions, the Chinese maintained their culture. Driven from the fields, replaced by the Japanese, Chinatown became a haven, not a battleground, for the Japanese and Chinese communities.

In 1899, in a major turnaround, the Chinese of Stockton were invited to take part in the 4th of July parade, signaling the beginning of a more tolerant attitude.

> The co-mingling of the entire population of Stockton at the great Fourth of July parade cemented an understanding between white and Chinese which transcended the confusion and frustrations of the anti-Chinese period of the 1880's. As 1899 ended both groups looked forward to closer and deeper relationships in the twentieth century...

The narration ends on a hopeful note. Slowly but surely, conditions improved for the Chinese of Stockton, due in large part to the efforts of Chinese women.

Sun Minnick describes the women's suffering. More importantly, she highlights the contributions of Chinese women to the community. With the 20th century and migration of women came the emphasis on family, tradition and education. "Changes in the community from a bachelor to a family society became apparent." Chinese-American women were independent and activist. Yet they faced difficult obstacles.

> As they helped support their families, these women discovered that work allowed them to be less dependent upon their husbands. Yet while work outside the home certainly expanded their social horizons, the independence they felt was bittersweet, for too often they were exhausted and drained from the double burden of working and raising a large family.

> Community activism among Chinese-American women was a natural consequence of the independence gained from years of working outside the home. In 1911 the Women's Young China Society was organized to support Dr. Sun Yat-Sen's revolution in China. These women related to the reforms Dr. Sun wished to make,

particularly the prohibition of footbinding and female infanticide. Many were on hand to hear his personal appeal during his visits to Stockton....

A myriad of organizations mediated disputes, supported democracy in China, raised money to help China after it was invaded by Japan. Chinese-Americans served in the U.S. Army. Minnick details both housing segregation and finally desegregation in the late 1950s and early 1960s. She details, too, the beginning of the end of Stockton's Chinatown.

The Stockton Chinese community, Minnick writes, is now heavily represented "in medicine, dental and professional fields...at work in all facets of the city and county's economy..." Minnick concludes with her hope for the future and her belief and pride in the Chinese of San Joaquin County who "have held steadfastly to their heritage but have in their forthright manner adopted western philosophical beliefs and lifestyles..."

Sylvia Sun Minnick has written an important book, contributing to both California literature and California history. The maps and photographs of Southern China and Northern California enrich the narrative. And one encounters, within a group history, moving individual portraits. One remembers the proud young Chinese who hangs himself in the county jail rather than go to San Quentin for a crime he did not commit. One is horrified by the suffering of Chinese women sold as prostitutes. One finds, recognized, the strong Chinese women now grown old, who in their time showed strength and courage, the women later elaborated on by Hong Kingston and Tan.

> With time and experience, these women developed a dauntless outlook and healthy self-esteem. While they were restricted from finding their own gold mountain, the wisdom and counsel they imparted gave their children the ability to perceive the winds of fortune. Despite all adversity and without others to show the way, these pioneering women became the role models for today's active Asian women.

Conclusion

California has changed in regard to racial prejudice. Perhaps we have taken two steps forward and—as of late—one step back.

I grew up in the Stockton of the late 1950s and 1960s. As a Jewish kid—recently arrived from Chicago—I, at times, heard and responded angrily to anti-Semitic remarks. For my Asian friends, it was worse. My neighborhood, Lincoln Village, restricted housing for Blacks and Asians until the early 1960s, and even after desegregation, sentiment was, for Blacks, despite many notable exceptions, racist. I felt in school that many of the students and teachers saw our neighborhood, city, state, and nation as a white Protestant Christian place. I was angry about it then and now while most whites have become more tolerant, one still cannot ignore the movement of some white kids toward Nazi skinhead groups. One can applaud progress but one cannot ignore the survival of white racism. And if the extreme right often posits a white Christian agenda, the radical left has also been racist and undemocratic. The solidarity of people of color is a myth and Chinese, Japanese, and Korean-Americans have suffered more from forms of affirmative action entitlements than have whites. Radicals have been especially insensitive to the suffering of Korean-Americans during and after the L.A. riots. In their lack of sympathy for the Koreans, we find echoes of labor's scapegoating of the Chinese over 120 years ago.

In the winter of 1974, I worked distributing newspapers. My route included Stockton's Chinatown; I dropped and counted bundles of papers for the paperboys in the silence of 3 A.M. Could I imagine the men, one hundred years gone, thousands of miles from home with solitary dreams of women, of longing and love? Could I imagine opium nightmares of dislocation, and doors forever closed, and loss? I could see only ghosts and shadows.

Sylvia Sun Minnick has filled in the shadows and given flesh to ghosts. She has given us back part of our history as Californians. For if we seek to ever live truly as a community in this state, then Chinese-California history is our history as well.

PART II

Three Greats

(from top left, clockwise) John Muir,
William Saroyan, John Steinbeck

CHAPTER 4

John Muir's California

"The whole state of California, from Siskiyou to San Diego, is one block of beauty, one matchless valley; and our great plain, with its mountain walls is the true California Yosemite—exactly corresponding in its physical character and proportions to that of the Merced."

— John Muir

John Muir is one of California's three essential writers. John Muir, William Saroyan and John Steinbeck are crucial to modern California literature. Saroyan's stories would be a model for all ethnic California writing, for Saroyan insisted upon both his ethnic and regional California identity. Steinbeck's indictment of social injustice would remind California authors that the physical beauty of our state must be complemented with communities that care for, in a compassionate way, those hurting in our midst. And John Muir, through his books and his life, saved our wilderness for future generations. Muir's books combine poetics with his own kind of activism. Like the Native Californians, Muir understood that nature must be cherished, not exploited. Muir's essays, thus, are works of literature that describe the beauty of our state and that, too, invite us to experience the beauty that Muir has described. Muir's writing would directly influence Wallace Stegner and Gary Snyder, David Brower, and the great Yosemite photographer, Ansel Adams, among many others. When we walk or hike the preserved wilderness of California, it is, in large part, thanks to the writing and life of John Muir.

Philosophy

John Muir, Scottish-born and Wisconsin-reared, was a seasoned naturalist and explorer by the time he arrived in California. In 1867, he began his now famous 1000-mile hike from Indianapolis to the Gulf of Mexico. Earlier, while an undergraduate at the University of Wisconsin, he had explored parts of Canada. By the time of his trek to the Gulf, he was a prose poet, a scientist and a religious man. According to University of Alaska professor Frank Ruske, "Muir carried to the Gulf the poems of Robert Burns, Milton's *Paradise Lost* and *The New Testament*." Already, Muir's thinking was 100 years ahead of his time. He had arrived, before the age of 30, to a crucial insight about humanity. He had written in his journal, "John Muir, Earth Planet, Universe." Also in his journal, he would write, "Why should man value himself as more than a small part of the great creation?" By the time Muir first stepped foot in Yosemite, he had become both a naturalist and a prose poet—who turned scientific observation into beautiful essays about nature. And Muir's observations about nature were firmly grounded in exact scientific observation.

His first published contribution, for example, on December 5, 1871, appeared in Horace Greeley's "New York Herald Tribune" entitled "Yosemite Glaciers." In that essay, Muir proved that "contrary to the conventional geological wisdom as expressed by Josiah Dwight Whitney of the California Geological Survey... the floor of Yosemite Valley had subsided during a series of cataclysmic events.... Muir found deposits of glacial silt... suggesting that the valley (from *Yosemite—The Embattled Wilderness* by Alfred Runte (page 48) had been shaped and scoured by successive waves of glaciers."

Yet, there was always much more than pure science in Muir's essays. If man was, as he wrote, "a small part of the great creation," humans were an essential portion of the creation, for we could appreciate and save nature for posterity. We could experience grace, Muir felt, not by dominating nature but by becoming one with it. Muir found God within nature.

> ...plain, sky, and mountains ray beauty which you
> feel. You bathe in these spirit-beams.... Presently you

lose consciousness of your own separate existence; you blend with the landscape and become part and parcel of nature.

Influenced by Ralph Waldo Emerson, Muir and Emerson became friends and, according to Frank Ruske, late in life, Emerson added Muir's name to his list of "My Men" (men who had the greatest effect on him). Unlike those men, Muir does not use the natural landscape to comment upon humanity, except by implication. Muir immerses the reader in the landscape so that we can appreciate our portion of the universe. We were, thought Muir, "a small part of the great creation," but our appreciation of the gift of light and mountains and rivers and life was not small, and Muir's essays are celebrations of the beauty he found and discovered in order to share with the rest of humanity.

Our Great Plain—The Central Valley

Muir was not a celebrator of California based on scant knowledge. He wrote about and explored Alaska and the Far West along with our state. He was drawn to California as his home because of the quality of the beauty of our entire geography. And so as early as 1872, in *The Overland Monthly*, the same magazine that Bret Harte had edited and Mark Twain had written for, Muir was to write out against what still, over 120 years later, is the idea that the Central Valley, called by Muir "our great plain," is a wasteland. Muir writes against this conception of the great valley.

From "Twenty Hill Hollow":

> ...in reading descriptions of California scenery by the *literary racers* [my emphasis] who annually make a trial of their speed here, one is led to fancy that, outside the touristical seesaw of Yosemite, Geysers, and Big Trees, our State contains little else worthy of note, excepting perhaps, certain wine-cellars and vineyards, and that our great plain is a sort of Sahara, whose narrowest and

least dusty crossing they benevolently light house. But to the few travelers who are in earnest—those lovers of the truth and beauty of wilderness—we would say, heed nothing you have heard. Those who submissively allow themselves to be packed and brined down in the sweats of a stage coach, who are herded into Yosemite by "favorite routes" are not aware that they are crossing a grander Yosemite than that to which they are going...

Muir is telling us to be aware and not race (or fly) across a landscape without being conscious of the country we have seen.

As I read Muir's passage about the valley, I remembered from my childhood the sudden clear winter days in Stockton that followed the rains, when we were aware again, in the absence of the fog, that we were in a true valley, the snowcapped majestic walls of the Sierra to the east, the purple Coast Range to the west, Mt. Diablo seeming close enough to touch; this landscape was still, then, as wondrous as Muir described. If we have lost some of this beauty, in the Central Valley and in the valleys of Southern California, it is because of the destruction of the environment, the cars, the industrial pollution, the overpopulation; for what beauty remains in our valleys, we can thank John Muir and the movement he helped to found.

Yosemite

We have been blessed with many excellent Yosemite painters and photographers, from Albert Bierstadt to Ansel Adams but no one, no painter or photographer, has equaled the descriptive powers of John Muir. Muir lived out Emerson's belief, expressed in the essay "Nature," that we should "enjoy an original relation to the universe." Emerson, in that essay, predicted Muir's character, "The lover of nature is he whose inward and outward senses are still truly adjusted to each other; who has retained the spirit of infancy even in the era of manhood. His intercourse with heaven and earth become part of his daily good. In the presence of

nature a wild delight runs through the man, in spite of real sorrows..."
Muir's philosophy is, I think, different from Emerson's and Thoreau's.
Both Emerson and Thoreau were social critics, often angry with the
mass of men, who, in Thoreau's words, "serve state not as men mainly but as machines with their bodies." Muir was an activist of another
kind. His readers are his companions, actually or vicariously hiking with
him in the Sierra; Muir's essays are based on the belief that his sharing,
through writing, the beauty of Yosemite and the Sierra, will lead us to
his conclusions. Once we experience Yosemite, through life or words,
how could we not save Yosemite?

Here, in the essay, "Yosemite Falls," Muir describes the falls, top,
bottom, and middle, from his perch 1400 feet above the valley floor. He
brings to us, his readers, "the afternoon sunshine... streaming through
the throng of comets, ever wasting, ever renewed."

At the top of the falls, Muir shows us the rushing water, "...they
all rush past us with amazing velocity and display of power...the heads
of these comet like masses are composed of nearly solid water, and are
dense white in color like pressed snow...while the outer finer sprays of
waterdust, whirling in sunny eddies, are pearly gray throughout..."

Muir describes the bottom of the falls, enclosing us in sight and
sounds. He describes:

> ...a hissing, flashing, seething...mass of scud and
> spray, through which the light sifts in gray and pur-
> ple tones, while at times, when the sun strikes at the
> required angle, the wild and apparently lawless mass is
> changed to brilliant rainbow hues, manifesting finest
> harmony.

The middle portion Muir feels is most beautiful—whose "rainbow
light makes divine." Muir concludes with a description of sound; the
falls have voice:

> ...its tones varying from the sharp hiss and rustle of the
> wind on the glossy leaves of the live oaks and the soft

sifting, hushing tones of the pines, to the loudest rush
and roar of storm winds and thunder among the crags
of the summit peaks.

Who, reading this essay, would not want to see Yosemite and who, seeing Yosemite, would not want to save Yosemite—and places like Yosemite—for our posterity?

Conclusion

"I care to live only to entice people to look at Nature's loveliness."
— *John Muir in a letter to his friend, Mrs. Ezra S. Carr*

As readers, we are like the painters in Muir's "Near View of the High Sierra," and Muir is our guide. The explorer writes of them and to us.

> I led them out of the valley by the Vernal and Nevada
> Falls.... They naturally were affected most by the col-
> ors—the intense azure of the sky, the purplish grays
> of the granite, the red and browns of the clay mead-
> ows and the translucent purple and crimson of huckle-
> berry...the flaming yellow of aspen, the silvery flashes
> of the streams, and the bright green and blue of the gla-
> cier lakes.

We could have no better guide. The National Park System and the preservation of Yosemite is, in great part, the result of Muir's meeting with President Theodore Roosevelt, who went camping with Muir in Yosemite. Muir fought to preserve the wilderness he loved. He was co-founder and first president of the Sierra Club. His work was the model for such men as Ansel Adams and David Brower. Beyond California, Muir would also have great importance. Literary historian Norman Foerster would write:

Whoever would know the Far West, from Alaska to Mexico, from the coast to the Rockies, must know John Muir...he gave this region to the country—both to those who would not go to see and to those who, having eyes, saw not. That is his foremost achievement.

It was in California that Muir, past 40, fell in love, married, fathered two daughters. He formed his roots in California. His descendants are more than his blood line. His efforts as writer and activist bore real fruit, and his fight is still necessary to continue today—against those who would despoil our most sacred gift of Nature.

CHAPTER 5

Saroyan's Legacy

"If I want to do anything I want to speak a more universal language...that which is eternal and common to all races."

—*William Saroyan*

California's greatest ethnic writer, in his lifetime, was many men. He was a son devastated by the early loss of his father, a child of Armenian immigrants and therefore a member of an oppressed people, a Fresno newsboy, a telegraph messenger, a high-school drop-out, a fieldworker, a San Francisco telegraph messenger, a dockworker, a bohemian, a drinker, a gambler, a playwright, an essayist, a short story writer, a storyteller, a novelist, a brother, son, uncle, failed husband, single father, a grandfather. William Saroyan was, as Gary Soto has written, one of the great writers of the century. He was, too, a personality, a force, a prose poet—colorful as Mark Twain, proud as Cyrano de Bergerac, with as much energy as a young Groucho Marx.

Saroyan was an ethnic writer long before the advent of ethnic literature courses. In a time of prejudice against Asian-Americans he reached out to help contemporaries like his Japanese-American friend Toshio Mori, helping Mori get his first book published. He wrote not only of immigrant Armenians but of American Greeks and Jews, Italians and Irish, Filipinos and Blacks, Arabs, Mexicans, Assyrians, Czechs, Poles, Russians, and Japanese. He wrote of Finland and New York and Armenia, but most of all he wrote of California, and he knew by intuition what those calling themselves multiculturalists today have yet to understand.

To write proudly about one's own people, Saroyan demonstrated, does not mean a lesser commitment to the many peoples of America. Writing from the inside of an ethnic culture, Saroyan illustrated, can lead one towards sympathy for other cultures. Indeed, ethnic awareness for Saroyan led him away from a stance of isolation and separatism and towards universal understandings.

Saroyan wrote of the joy and pain of childhood, the poignancy of time's passage; he argued again and again that accepting our mortality, our closeness to death, should lead us towards lives of dignity and honor. From his first published book in 1934 when he was 26 to his last published work before his death in 1981 at the age of 72, Saroyan published more than 40 volumes of stories, plays, essays, novels, and autobiographies. Of his more than 500 stories, I will focus on four of Saroyan's most telling pieces, those illustrating his world—a place where one can be, simultaneously, fully ethnic, fully American, fully human.

The Stories

"The Filipino and the Drunkard" is one of Saroyan's strongest stories. Those who have read only a little of Saroyan, *The Human Comedy* or *My Name is Aram*, will be surprised, I think, by the controlled anger behind the story, based on a true-life incident that happened on the San Francisco-to-Oakland ferry "before the Bay Bridge was built." It is a story that fully exposes racist evil and indicts those who stand by while evil takes place.

A World War I veteran, enraged at the presence of a nonwhite on the deck of a ferry, begins to torment a young Filipino. The veteran's racism is made explicit, and Saroyan shows how false patriotism often serves as a mask for super nationalism. The veteran states, "Now get back...I fought twenty-four months in France. I'm a real American. I don't want you standing here among white people."

The veteran drunkenly chases the Filipino into the washroom, threatening the young man's life. None of the passengers on the ferry intervene and the Filipino, in self-defense, uses his knife to kill his assailant.

The Filipino's final speech is an indictment of all who stand by while the innocent are oppressed.

I did not want to hurt him. Why didn't you stop him? Is it right to chase a man like a rat? You knew he was drunk. I did not want to hurt him, but he would not let me go. He tore my coat and tried to choke me. I told him I would kill him if he would not go away. It is not my fault. I must go to Oakland to see my brother. He is sick. Do you think I am looking for trouble when my brother is sick? Why didn't you stop him?

Here is a story totally applicable to our racial situation today. During the past years, we have heard justification for both the Rodney King and Reginald Denny beatings. Those who did the right thing, the white policewoman who wept in court and admitted shame and wrong in regard to the unnecessary blows to King—and the African-Americans who saved Denny—are not celebrated. Instead, white racists justify King's beating, even though King was struck after clearly being subdued, and Black racists justify what happened to Denny, a man innocent of any crime, victimized only because of his white skin. Meanwhile, others explain away the violence done to Korean-Americans as if they are not equally—with all of us in the United States—deserving of full protection under the law.

Saroyan, in "The Filipino and the Drunkard," shows us that being a bystander to evil and doing nothing is to be an accessory to evil. He shows us, further, that bigotry based on race is totally indefensible.

Saroyan's ability to write about ethnic groups different from his own is especially compelling. His Armenian experience—two million of his people murdered at the hands of the Turks—and his Armenian-American experience, in his hometown of Fresno; Armenians were restricted in housing until after World War II—moved Saroyan to identify with other victims of prejudice.

"The Broken Wheel" is told from within a close Armenian-American family in Fresno. The story is not straight autobiography but is, like many of Saroyan's stories, based on Saroyan's true-life situation.

Saroyan's mother, following the death of her husband, raised a family of four children, two girls and two boys, with a courage that did not mask the essential tragedy of the family situation. Mrs. Sandoval, the Mexican-American woman who loses her son in *The Human Comedy* and Mrs. McCauley, the Irish-American widow in the same novel, are projections of Saroyan's mother.

Saroyan's Armenian-American stories are grounded in ethnic detail and Saroyan provides us with Armenian names and phrases, but the impact of "The Broken Wheel" relies on the poignance of the family situation—of a family sobered by death, unbowed by poverty, untied by love.

The story's key figure is the mother, a young widow. Despite the loss of the father, the family is a happy one, but the happiness is touched by an awareness of sorrow. The youngest child, a boy, narrates, "In the winter we laughed a great deal. We would be sullen and sorrowful for weeks at a time and then suddenly all of us would begin to laugh..."

In the summer, the mother's brother, Uncle Vahan, would visit. An immigrant, young Vahan has already become an attorney in San Francisco. He tells the family, "We do not know how fortunate we are to be in a country such as this. Opportunities are unlimited..."

Vahan speaks with happiness and confidence, but Saroyan will bring us, here, the opposite of the sentimental American success story.

Tragedy visits the family again. First, a seemingly meaningless event takes on great meaning for the narrator. The brothers, for years, have shared a bicycle, the older brother pumping the younger brother, who sits on the crossbars. One afternoon the fork cracks and the author describes the break as a sudden awareness of the passage of time, as a sort of death and rebirth; when the fork breaks he experiences it as "coming out of an endless dream."

The narrator suddenly is conscious of himself and his family becoming older, of his two sisters' love for the family and his brother and his times of growing up. He remembers "the time I nearly drowned in the Kings River and Krikor swam after me shouting frantically in Armenian. The time Lucy lost her job at Woolworth's and cried a week. The time Naomi was ill with pneumonia and we all prayed she wouldn't die..."

The story concludes with the family learning of Uncle Vahan's death in World War I and with the narrator describing his mother, who has told the tearful children, "We have always had our disappointments and hardships and we have always come out of them and we always shall." The narrator awakens from sleep at night and observes his mother's suffering:

> I saw that my mother had taken her brother's photograph from the piano. She had placed it before her on the table and I could hear her weeping softly, and I could hear her swaying her head from side to side the way people from the old country do...

If ever a story acknowledges the strength of women, this one does. If ever a story is both an ethnic and universal rendering, this one is.

"The Death of Children" integrates Saroyan's Armenian-American experience with the experience of other ethnic Americans. In his collection, "The Man with the Heart in the Highlands," Saroyan's familiarity with the cultures around him allowed him to write of a Greek waiter in "The Struggle of Jim Patros with Death," an Italian-American schoolboy in "Laughter," an Oklahoma migrant family in "Oranges," African-Americans in "Peace, It's Wonderful," and American Indians in "The Third Day After Christmas." An important story of the 1930s, "With a Hey Nonny Nonny" sympathetically described a Mexican-American farmworker involved in a strike. In several stories published before World War II, culminating with his Pulitzer Prize winning play, *The Time of Your Life*, Saroyan made the fate of Europe's Jewish population a specific concern. His own people had suffered genocide, and he understood early on the meaning of Nazi brutality and racism.

In "The Death of Children" Saroyan recalls his fourth grade class. He portrays the multi-ethnic nature of his class in a single sentence— "There were all kinds of us"—and then describes two girls and two boys of his class.

There was Rose Tapia, "the little Mexican girl," who Saroyan remembers as representing "the rhythm of song." There is Carson, the

Southern migrant boy, who lived with his parents "in a tent somewhere south of the S.P. tracks," who because of poverty came "to school in the winter without shoes." The other boys taunt the migrant, who becomes mean and sullen, but Saroyan is convinced that Carson was ashamed of his meanness.

There is Alice Schwab, the teacher's favorite, the daughter of a Jewish watchmaker, who dies tragically that year in the flu epidemic. And finally, there is the Armenian boy, witness to massacre, whom Saroyan identifies as his brother. The Armenian boy speaks to Saroyan in Armenian during recess and tells him of what he has witnessed, of what their people have suffered:

> ...and their house was burning, and he could see men being struck by soldiers with whips and blades and he could hear screaming and praying...and then they killed his father before his eyes, and his mother became insane with grief...and along the roads he saw the bodies of dead men and women and the bodies of dead children, and all over the country it was the same, and everywhere were the bodies of children who had died...

Here, Saroyan is like the Jewish writers who, after the Holocaust, have seen it as an obligation to tell the truth of what took place. Reading this story, our students, Vietnamese- and Cambodian-American future writers, might find a way of eventually giving voice to the horrors they have seen.

"70,000 Assyrians" is perhaps Saroyan's most compelling statement about ethnicity, American assimilation, and brotherhood. The story is set in 1933 at the Barber College on Third Street in San Francisco's skid row. It is the height of the Depression and at the Barber College Saroyan meets a number of suffering men. There is a kid he calls "Iowa" who is out of work, hungry, far from his native Midwest, looking desperately for any kind of job, looking for a place in the world. There is the Japanese-American barber with whom Saroyan quickly establishes rapport, for Saroyan exchanges words with the barber in Japanese, words he had learned working in the fields years before. The Japanese-American barber and Saroyan have mutual friends. Finally, Saroyan meets the Assyrian barber, Theodore Badal, who Saroyan first mistakes as a fellow Armenian. Badal and Saroyan speak to each other and Saroyan becomes discouraged, perceiving that Badal has lost himself spiritually by giving up on his Assyrian ancestry. "Badal said, 'I cannot read Assyrian. I was born in the old country but I want to get over it.'"

Saroyan comments: "These remarks were very painful to me, an Armenian. I had always felt badly about my own people being destroyed…"

Badal tells Saroyan that there are only 70,000 Assyrians left in the world "…and the Arabs are still killing us. They killed 70 of us in a little uprising last month. Seventy more destroyed…" Saroyan, who has not given up hope for an independent Armenia, sees Badal, despite himself, representing his people, "himself 70,000 Assyrians, and still being himself, the whole race…" He does not accept that Badal has given up on his ancestry.

Saroyan embraces here the hope that we can retain our ethnicity and yet be fully American. His idea of America was of a place encompassing many cultures, a haven to the oppressed, a place of justice something Whitmanesque, out of Lincoln. Saroyan's America was the place articulated by Emma Lazarus in her poem on the Statue of Liberty; it was the place Martin Luther King dreamed of and Robert Kennedy campaigned for. It is a vision of the United States that we should not let die.

Saroyan wrote many stories, of many kinds, most less tragic than the four I've discussed here. He was consistent always in his respect for other cultures and his feeling for the fragility of life. Sadly, except for *My Name is Aram* and *The Human Comedy*, Saroyan's work is mainly out of print, so the interested reader will have to find individual stories in anthologies, used bookstores, and libraries. Collections such as *The Daring Young Man on the Flying Trapeze*, *The Man with his Heart in the Highlands*, *The Saroyan Special*, and *The Whole Voyald* are filled with Saroyan's prose, poetry, humanity, and humor. ABC has aired Saroyan's "The Paisley Garden," adapted by Henry Saroyan, the author's nephew, and narrated by James Earl Jones. It was a fine adaptation, consistent with the story. According to Henry Saroyan, as quoted in the *San Francisco Chronicle*, other of his uncle's stories may be adapted for ABC.

"Miraculously Living Things"

In our time of bitterness and polemics, reading Saroyan might help restore our appreciation of the eternal truths. We need to expand, not limit, our ideas about culture and ethnicity. Anyone who calls himself or herself a multiculturalist and sees all those of European ancestry as the same is simply spreading bigotry. Further, to the extent multiculturalists deny the tremendous diversity and individuality among members of every ethnic group, denial will be a measure of failure.

In late June of 1993, I spent eleven days at Kaiser Hospital in Hayward after undergoing successful major surgery. My surgeon, to whom I owe much, was Dr. Peterson, a Swedish-American originally from Visalia. My grandparents are Russian Jews who fled *pogroms* to come to the United States; and my late grandfather, the sculptor Joseph Gilden, lost relatives in the Holocaust. My roommates, all bravely facing serious diagnoses, included a Filipino World War II veteran, a Latino father of two young children, an Air Force Vietnam-era veteran who is one-quarter Native-American, and a retired Naval captain, from Harlan County, Kentucky, who took part in the Normandy invasion.

My nurses, all caring, were black, white, Hispanic, Filipino, Chinese, and other nationalities. With the doctors, nurses, and my fellow patients, our ethnicity was, at times, a topic of conversation but never the focus of relationship. All of us shared, it seemed to me, an awareness of the closeness of death and an appreciation of life, in the face of that reality.

We live in a more multicultural society than the multiculturalists admit. Our society, in many ways, has transcended race. A multiculturalism that does not explore our common humanity betrays the essence of literature. For we are, to again quote Saroyan, all of us, individual human beings, "miraculously living things, never more than a day from death, never far from glory."

CHAPTER 6

Steinbeck's Compassion

"…Everybody wants a little bit of land, not much. Just som'thin' that was him. Somethin' he could live on and there couldn't nobody throw him off it. I never had none. I planted crops for damn near ever'body in this state but they wasn't my crops and when I harvested 'em, it wasn't none of my harvest."

—*Candy's speech from John Steinbeck's* Of Mice and Men

I t was fall, Indian summer, when I began this essay, which will not appear until spring. Now it has become cold autumn, winter is coming on, and the news of the devastation from the fires of Southern California already is becoming a memory.

Of Mice and Men is a work I like to teach in hot, late September. The mood of the novella fits the end of summer though the author, himself, does not name the season. The third paragraph states only that it is "…Evening of a hot day…." Yet the mood of the book is a September, coastal California mood and the novel's tragic, sudden climax ends a brief season of heat and hope.

John Steinbeck was California's greatest author. What John Muir understood about nature in Yosemite, what Jack London found in Oakland's streets and waterfront, what Frank Norris detailed in Central Valley injustice, and what William Saroyan knew about the dreams of California's immigrants, Steinbeck integrated into his greatest work. Without John Steinbeck, writers as different as Luis Valdez, Gerald Haslam, Joan Didion, Richard Rodriguez, Tillie Olsen, Hisaye Yamamoto—as well as the great photographer Dorothea Lange—could not as readily have found location, definition, and voice.

Steinbeck, grandson of German and Irish immigrants, understood the meaning of California. His country is a place of longing, turmoil, and hope, a scene of the best and worst dreams and actions of human-kind. He saw California, to quote Robert Penn Warren, as a place in the world of possible renewal, "...the scene of a new chance for man and men." Wrote Warren,

> ...Steinbeck is not only continuing an American tradition, enacting again an old American dream. He is also suggesting that the dream itself has moved west ...that it is now California which stimulates in its inhabitants the intoxicating sense of fresh beginnings and untroubled potentialities which the Eastern scene once stimulated in Emerson, in Thoreau, in Whitman ...

When our dream of new beginnings ends in suffering and violence, one feels, within Steinbeck's prose poetry, a betrayal of humanity itself.

The 1930s was the decade of Steinbeck's greatness, the decade when, within the suffering of the Depression, America found in California its greatest artist. *The Grapes of Wrath* came at decade's end; it is Steinbeck's greatest novel, and I would place alongside that novel Steinbeck's non-fiction masterpiece first published as *Their Blood is Strong*, reissued fifty years later as *The Harvest Gypsies*—based on the reportage that became fictionalized in *The Grapes of Wrath*. *The Long Valley*, published in 1937, collects most of Steinbeck's important short fiction, including "The Chrysanthemums," "Breakfast," "Leader of the People," and "Flight." *In Dubious Battle*, an earlier novel than *The Grapes of Wrath*, is a strike novel that combines analysis of head with feeling of heart. Anyone interested in the labor scene of the 1930s should read *In Dubious Battle*, the work of a man of the left who was not Stalinist, never totalitarian.

Of Mice and Men was first published in 1937. Specifically noted in Steinbeck's Nobel Price citation, it is still the author's most teachable work. As a novella, play, and screenplay, it communicates on a series of levels to students of all ages, from junior high school on. During the Steinbeck festival of 1991, I watched the Watts Theater Company, composed of young black and Latino actors and actresses, perform the play. When the cast took questions, after the performance, a member of the audience asked why it was Steinbeck they had chosen to perform. A young Latina actress spoke: "Because I felt John Steinbeck was a man who would have loved and understood my grandfather's life."

A black actor explained how much the character of Crooks had moved him. The writer, the creator, had touched their hearts. It was fitting, I felt, watching the play, that the company should perform Steinbeck—for the author had been, following the 1965 riots, one of the original financial contributors to Budd Schulberg's Watts Writer's Workshop. Steinbeck was a man who, in his writing as in his life, saw past color and race to the essence of human hope and desire.

The Novella Itself

Of Mice and Men has power because it is about the struggles of individual human beings. Lennie Small is not only a representative of the mentally handicapped; he is depicted as one man imprisoned within his handicap, unable to channel his great strength or his equally strong, loving heart. Similarly, Curly's wife is a lonely, tormented, cruel young woman; and she also is, by the novel's conclusion, a true victim. We will grieve over a man and a woman as well as a lost dream. In a very real way Steinbeck, here, as in his other major works, mourns the unborn world, the world that should have been, could have been, but because of human blindness, greed, selfishness, and fate, never was.

Steinbeck sets the novel in his native county and exhibits, as always, an absolute mastery of setting and place.

> A few miles south of Soledad, the Salinas River drops
> in close to the hillside bank and runs deep and green
> ...There is a path through the willows and among the
> sycamores ...beaten down hard by tramps who come
> wearily down from the highway on the evening...

Characters are defined through dialogue, through the hard poetry of American speech. Listen as George Milton explains to the sympathetic mule skinner Slim how he became Lennie's surrogate brother, father, protector, friend, how cruelty turned to compassion.

> "...I used to have a hell of a lot of fun with 'im. Used to play jokes on 'im 'cause he was too dumb to take care of 'imself. But he was too dumb even to know he had a joke played on him. I had fun. Made me seem God damn smart alongside of him. Why he'd do any damn thing I tol' him. If I tol' him to walk over a cliff, over he'd go. That wasn't so damn much fun after a while. He never got mad about it, neither. I've beat the hell outa him, and he coulda bust every bone in my body jus' with his han's, but he never lifted a finger against me." George's voice was taking on the tone of confession. "Tell you what made me stop that. One day a bunch of guys was standin' around on the Sacramento River. I was feelin' pretty smart. I turns to Lennie and says, 'Jump in.' An' he jumps. Couldn't swim a stroke. He damn near drowned before we could get him. An' he was so damn nice to me for pullin' him out. Clean forgot I told him to jump in. Well, I ain't done nothing like that no more."

Slim's response shows his understanding of Lennie's essence as well as his understanding of George's love for his friend: "Sure he's jes like a kid. There ain't no more harm in him than a kid either, except he's so strong..."

It will be Lennie's strength, not his retardation, that will cause the novella's tragedy, though it is society's reaction to his retardation that has formed Lennie's character and underlined his fears—the very fears that lead him to unintentional murder.

While all the film versions of *Of Mice and Men* have power, watching the movie should not be a substitute for reading and rereading the novella. Each reading makes one more aware of the richness of detail, of the way Steinbeck fills in a scene, of his knowledge of people. A minor character like Whit gives the novel resonance. When Whit reacts to the shooting of Candy's dog—"What the hell's taking him so long?"—one hears the voice of complicity, of guilt. In the novel, Candy's speeches become Depression poetry; one is aware that this is a book that came out of suffering life.

> "You seen what they done to my dog tonight? They say he wasn't no good to himself nor nobody else. When they came here I wisht somebody'd shoot me. But they won't."

George's speeches to Lennie are easy to caricature, but a close reading takes one beyond the caricature. George's speech is actually a variation upon a theme, and each variation affords a richness of imagery.

> "...I could build a smoke house like the one gran'pa had.... An' when salmon run up river we could catch a hundred of 'em and salt 'em down or smoke 'em. We could have them for breakfast. They ain't nothing so nice as smoked salmon. When the fruit come in we could can it—and tomatoes, they're easy to can. Ever' Sunday we'd kill a chicken or a rabbit. Maybe we'd have a cow or a goat, and the cream is so God damn thick you got to cut it with a knife and take it out with a spoon."

George and Lennie's speeches rehearse dreams of the future, while Steinbeck's understanding of the crippling effects of racism detail the present. Steinbeck's knowledge of his characters is based on close observation of how people act and talk.

Crooks's retaliation to white racism is to strike out against Lennie, the only white he can vent his anger upon safely: "They say I stink. Well, I tell you, you all stink to me." That Crooks finds hope—before he is victimized and threatened by Curly's wife—gives meaning to the secondary tragedy within the novella. Candy has become a believer and participant in George and Lennie's dream, so much so that he has broken through the wall of racism and invited Crooks to join the other men, and become a partner at the dream ranch.

George has not quite understood, and will not, perhaps until Lennie's death, the bonds that join all humankind. His first impulse is to exclude Crooks. That George excludes Crooks without malice does not detract from the hurt it delivers to the black man. Yet one is never sure that George would not have changed his mind. Crooks makes George's rejection final.

"Member what I said about hoein' and doin' odd jobs?"

"Yeah," said Candy. "I remember."

"Well, jus' forget it," said Crooks. "I didn't mean it. Jus' foolin.' I wouldn't want to go to no place like that."

Of Mice and Men deals, too, with the mistreatment and cruel use of women. Steinbeck handles this issue in his own manner, in a way that is forceful without being polemical. Steinbeck has not been celebrated enough for his portraits of women. An early story, "Molly Morgan" from *The Pastures of Heaven,* is a heartbreaking, sensitive study of a Salinas Valley young woman schoolteacher, devastated by the reappearance of her father, who had been thought dead but had, in fact, deserted the family. Likewise, Eliza of "The Chrysanthemums" is a full-blooded woman, as sympathetic as any in American short fiction. Mrs. Joad in *The Grapes of Wrath* and Juana of *The Pearl* are as real as the male characters. Without Steinbeck's strong female characters, the male characters would be rendered meaningless.

Curly's wife, like Lennie, is a person victimized by the time in which she lives. Unlike Lennie, her dreams are pitiful Hollywood dreams. Also, unlike Lennie, she has acted cruelly, hurt Crooks badly, set in motion forces beyond her control. Her death, at Lennie's hands, restores her to dignity. In death, Steinbeck writes: "...And the meanness and plannings and the ache for attention were all gone from her face. She was very pretty and simple and her face was sweet and young."

Steinbeck's short novel remains true to the dual qualities the author charged writers to address in his Nobel Address, "to expose our many grievous faults and failings..." and to, also, "declare and celebrate man's proven capacity...for gallantry in defeat, for courage, compassion and love." Steinbeck wrote tragically, not to demean humankind but as one who believed, to again quote from the Nobel Address, "passionately...in the perfectibility of man."

Notes Toward a Conclusion

Some lessons that we learn young are false lessons; others are lessons that we take with us forever. *Of Mice and Men* is a work that can be read first in junior high school, again in high school, and later in adult life. It is an honest, tragic work.

My surgeon spoke to me in the hospital last August about the delayed effect the novella had on him. He had read the book in high school, half remembering it; twenty-five years later he saw the 1992 version of the film on an airplane, flying to the East. "When Candy's dog was shot," my doctor told me, "I remembered everything, and I felt the way I feel when I lose a patient. I feel hopeless, despite all I've wanted and tried to do."

The version of the film I like to show students is the version with Robert Blake as George, Dennis Quaid as Lennie, made for NBC in the late 1980s. Quaid's acting gets across Lennie's basic warmth and tenderness. In Quaid's characterization and Blake's response, we see the potential of a dream that could have happened, should have happened—that has happened now, in part, for thousands of retarded citizens today—thanks to the efforts and care for many good men and women.

Starting at 3 P.M., mentally disabled women and men walk home from the activity center, a half block from my apartment. My sister, Mimi, gone now twelve years this January, went to such a center, where she learned to make things of beauty with her hands. How can I find the words to describe my sister? How much she loved us—my brother and me, out mother and father, our grandparents. How much she was a friend to her friends. How she smiled and laughed. How she felt profoundly for others, beyond the words she had to describe her feelings. How she loved life.

Why do I honor John Steinbeck's memory? Because I know he would have felt for my sister, understood her struggle with a seizure disorder, identified with her bravery and pain. It is impossible to conceive of American or California literature without John Steinbeck and his hope, humor, anger against injustice, and finally—his compassion.

"This world was lucky," as Woody Guthrie said of President Roosevelt, "to see him born."

PART III

The Depression and World War II

(from top left, clockwise) Son of depression refugee from Oklahoma now in California, World War II poster, newspaper headlines announcing Japanese relocation, Oakland, CA (1942)

CHAPTER 7

Depression Legacies

Horace McCoy and Charles Bukowski

Horace McCoy

Horace McCoy's view of life is polar opposite to John Steinbeck's. His 1935 novel, *They Shoot Horses, Don't They?* and his view of Depression-era Los Angeles gives voice to the California that is not a promised land. Like Charles Bukowski after him and like Nathaniel West of his own time, Los Angeles, for McCoy, is a place defined by our worst dreams. The image of California projected by McCoy is a counter to the viewpoint that sees our state as a place of human possibility. The split between California as a place of hope and California as a geography of despair would continue into the 1960s and resurface during the decade of the 1990s.

During the 1960s, forceful ideas supporting social change among the counterculture would exist alongside apocalyptic visions fueled by drugs, visions leading to suicide and murder. Haight Street and Telegraph Avenue contained young people whose desire was to peacefully change themselves and society, as well as people who would come to the most violent conclusions. Were the 1960s about flower children and love or about Charles Manson and Hell's Angels murdering at the Altamont?

And are the contemporary young adults we see on the street abused kids whose tattoos, body piercings and angry attitude mask a real sensitivity, or are these young people destroying themselves and terrorizing others in a revenge for "a world I never made"?

From the Depression on, California literature has divided itself between those who have seen California as a final hope for community and justice and those other writers who have found in California a final bitter joke.

Horace McCoy, like Nathaniel West and like Bukowski, can find here no redemption. Yet McCoy's *They Shoot Horses, Don't They?* is, in its own way, as radical as anything by Steinbeck or Upton Sinclair. McCoy's depiction of a dance marathon is a projection of an American travesty and tragedy. In a short, compelling narration we meet a number of young Americans who have come to Los Angeles to pursue dreams that are both totally unrealistic and typically American. The narrator, Robert, wants to be a film director. His dance partner, Gloria, wants to be an actress. Like Curly's wife in Steinbeck's *Of Mice and Men*, the dream is both pathetic and oddly touching. For McCoy, like Steinbeck, has not created these characters in order to make fun of them.

Young women abused in Middle America or the South come to Hollywood, where they gamble their youth and sexuality against possibilities for a future life. Fans crowd an arena in Santa Monica to watch the marathon dancers who compete for a prize of $1,000 destroy themselves in some American counterpoint to the Mexican bullfight—the dancers not brave bulls but young men and women dying physically and emotionally as they chase not a bullfighter but a cash prize and a dream of glory.

In the month and more that is the space of the narrative, McCoy describes stabbings, passionless sex, murder—and a finale where Robert, the novel's narrator, shoots Gloria, his dance partner—at her own request.

Gloria has seen through her own dreams, and after McCoy narrates the story of her life, after the 879 hours on the dance floor and the speeches she delivers about her former life, the novel's conclusion makes a kind of eerie, logical common sense.

Here, Gloria and Robert give their final exchange. Gloria speaks first:

> "...Anyway, I'm finished. I think it's a lousy world and I'm finished. I'd be better off dead and so would everybody else..."

> I did not say anything, listening to the ocean slosh against the pilings, feeling the pier rise and fall, and thinking she was right about everything she had said.

> Gloria was fumbling in her purse. When her hand came
> out it was holding a small pistol. I had never seen the
> pistol before, but I was not surprised. I was not in the
> least surprised. "Here," she said, offering it to me.

In his foreword to the screenplay, Sydney Pollack, who directed the compelling film version of the novel, lets us know that the first director to express interest in the novel was Charlie Chaplin. How would Chaplin have found humanity in a scene that has none? Could Chaplin, a film genius, have done the story without changing McCoy's point of view?

For none of McCoy's characters is likeable. The older wealthy woman "fan" who "helps" Robert and Gloria find a sponsor wants to keep and use Robert sexually. Gloria has given herself to the promoter and, as usual, advanced her life not an inch. Couples fall, have heart attacks, collapse under the strain. A fake marriage is proposed and promoted. Movie stars and starlets show up not to case suffering but as a publicity stunt to lubricate their own careers. And the marathon end with a shooting and no winner, no prize. And Robert, when he shoots Gloria is, of course, murdering himself as well.

McCoy's view of life, told so matter-of-factly, is unremitting. Yet the reader remembers touching moments from the novel. I remember Robert, trying to dance with Gloria, toward a square of sunlight. In another vivid scene Robert, in the locker room, sees the ocean outside the door and feels a sudden surge of hope in the place he, like an animal, is trapped in. Those touches humanize an otherwise joyless narration.

Our greatest California writers, I believe, contrary to McCoy, give us the hope that life is more than a cycle of meaninglessness and pain.

Yet McCoy has created a work of art, and one that will stay contemporary for so long as the mass media, the entertainment industry, is involved in the exploitation of humanity. And in California—how many since the 1930s have entered our big cities—Los Angeles and San Francisco—only to enter a graveyard? Many have dreamed the most shallow of California dreams—to be a movie star, a performer, a singer, a dancer, and this has been for a talentless multitude, their final dream. McCoy's strength is that he does not condescend to these people. A shallow dream does not efface deep suffering. His pair of marathon dancers finally know they have been exploited, and this understanding makes the novel not farce but close to tragedy itself.

Bukowski's *Post Office*

During the 1960s and until his death in 1994, Charles Bukowski detailed a Los Angeles whose hopelessness mirrored Horace McCoy's.

Bukowski, now so much imitated, was an original, one of that type described by Edward Dahlberg as a "bottom dog." Born in 1920 in Germany, he was brought by his parents to Los Angeles at the age of three, and although he lived in many U.S. cities, Los Angeles was always his home. His writing hero was Italian-American novelist John Fante, a friend of William Saroyan whose novels include *Wait Until Spring Bandini, The Road to Los Angeles,* and *Bunker Hill.* From Fante, Bukowski learned how a novel could be told in the writer's own speaking voice, vernacular speech used to shape and control the action of fiction. For Bukowski that voice is the one of the unrepentant alcoholic, bar fighter, womanizer, street poet. Sometimes Bukowksi's novels are mere repetitions of his drinking and sexual exploits. But at his best, and *Post Office* is among his best, Bukowski is a poet of Los Angeles's lower depths, a man who really lived the life that his middle- and upper-class bohemian imitators have, at best, only played with.

Post Office begins in the late 1950s and ends in 1970. The novel covers the years Bukowski worked for the U.S. Post Office in Los Angeles. There are sections embedded in the novel that show an unsentimental sympathy for the working man trapped in a dead-end job. At times the novel echoes themes found in Jack London as well as Horace McCoy. The writer has seen how the social machine works and destroys. That this destruction happens amid palm trees and warm skies makes the tragedy no less compelling.

Bukowksi, in the following passage, made me remember some of the men and women I knew and worked with in the main Oakland Post Office. This passage is bitterly true. Writes Bukowski of a colleague:

Eleven years shot through the head. I had seen the job eat men up. They seemed to melt. There was Jimmy Potts at Dorsey Station. When I first came in, Jimmy had been a well-built guy in a white t-shirt. Now he was gone. He put his seat as close to the floor as possible and braced himself from falling over his feet...He walked very slow...They had murdered him. He was 55. He had seven years until retirement.

"I'll never make it," he told me.

And there I was, dizzy spells, and pain in the arms, neck, chest, everywhere. I slept all day resting up for the job...

For these workers, working under the circumstances of difficulty year in, year out required overtime, night after night; the cancellation of days off; the sadistic bosses; the cruel supervisors; Los Angeles is just another big American city. Under these conditions the dream of California, the ocean, the sunlight, the beautiful people on the street, is just a mirage. Bukowski, through guts and luck and talent as a writer, broke out of a particular California nightmare. *Post Office* is about those who remain. And if the Post Office has been reformed since the author's time—what of the men and women and children working in California's illegal sweatshops, at jobs far below minimum wage—while others walk in sunshine and light? For those people, the cities of California are cruel cities and the promise of California is only a shattered hope.

CHAPTER 8

Nightmare Prophecies and Visions of Hope

Nathaniel West and Tillie Olsen

Nathaniel West

"...Across the top, parallel with the frame, he had drawn the burning city, a great bonfire of architectural styles, ranging from Egyptian to Cape Cod Colonial. Through the center, winding from left to right was a long hill street and down it, spilling into the middle foreground, came the mob, carrying baseball bats and torches. For the faces of its members he was using the innumerable sketches of the people who had come to California...all those poor devils who can only be stirred by the promise of miracles and only then to violence... No longer bored they sang and danced in the red light of the flames."

—Nathaniel West, The Day of the Locust, *1939*

"Sally and Ron, a Minnesota farm couple in their 30s, were here this week taking what's fast becoming known locally as 'the O.J. tour.'

"They paid $1,300 in airfare and hotel bills to spend two days visiting sites made famous in the O.J. Simpson murder case and they weren't going to be stopped by a little thing like the yellow tape marking police lines...when they came to 875 where Nicole Brown Simpson lived and where she and her waiter friend Ron Goldman died, their disposable camera came out.

"'I just had to see what kind of house she lived in,' said Sally..."

—Oakland Tribune, June 29, 1994

"...The orgiastic crowd, loving you this moment, destroying you the next, is the essence of Hollywood—as Hollywood may be the essence of our success-driven culture...."

—*Budd Schulberg, from Introduction to*
The Day of the Locust, *Time-Life edition, 1965*

Nathaniel West's *The Day of the Locust,* strong as it is, is not the defining work of California literature. It lacks the connection to place and sympathy for others that is the hallmark of our greatest California works, from Steinbeck's *The Grapes of Wrath* and William Saroyan's *The Time of Your Life* to Hisaye Yamamoto's *Seventeen Syllables* and Tillie Olsen's *Tell Me a Riddle.* Yet some critics, beginning with Edmund Wilson in "The Boys in the Back Room," have elevated West as a way of dismissing California literature, and indeed California life itself.

But just as West should not be used to diminish other California writers, those other writers should not be used to diminish West's achievement. *The Day of the Locust* is of undeniable power and importance. If it is not the major California novel, it is a major California novel. Classic and still contemporary, it is honest in its anger and bitterness. It is a half-vision, but a brilliant half-vision, and recent events have demonstrated again how terribly prophetic West really was.

West captured, better than anyone, how Hollywood's disease reflects a national sickness. West understood, 55 years before the Simpson case, our fascination with lurid detail, our ability to be part of a mob, our desire for gossip and dirt—all fed by the tabloid press and media superstructure.

And how easy it is, now, to congratulate oneself for watching Peter Jennings or Tom Brokaw or Dan Rather, instead of Geraldo or Donahue or Maury Povich. But can any of us say, at this point, where Geraldo ends and Dan Rather begins? We rest our honor upon slender threads. Which of us has not become an amateur psychologist, pontificating happily, as two more innocents lie dead?

The Thin Line

West's hero, Tod Hackett, is a painter, a talented young artist who has come to Hollywood from the East to work as a designer of film sets. Tod believes he can be detached, create art, and observe evil while remaining untouched by evil. He is wrong, and West uses Tod's fall to illustrate that there is a thin line between observation and complicity. By novel's end Tod has become witness to a murder; he has been reduced to a would-be rapist; he has become a rejected boyfriend of a beautiful but vicious girl-woman. He is finally a man screaming, as in a painting by Munch, in imitation of a police car siren as a mob riots, not in legitimate anger but in joyous carnival.

He has deluded himself as so many have since.

> ...He told himself that it didn't make any difference because he would not be judged by the accuracy which it [his painting] foretold the future but by its merit as a painting....

Tod has told himself that he could escape the nightmare of immorality around him by remaining an observer and by judging through his art.

The novel's perspective is Tod's, and though Tod does not consider himself an innocent, he is naïve, for every single character is more depraved than Tod had believed—they are not just lonely, not grotesques, but true monsters. Homer Simpson is not merely an Iowa hick; once betrayed, he becomes a violent killer, stomping to death a demonic child actor. Fay Greener, whom Tod loves and thinks of as a lost girl, is, at age 18, a hardened prostitute, a prototype for past, present, and future Heidi Fleisses. Fay's lovers, a Texas cowboy and a Mexican promoter of cockfights, are not tough, colorful Westerners, but brutal and evil men. The dwarf Abe Kusich is clearly every bit as deformed in mind as in body. And Tod's friend, the producer who calls his Chinese houseboy a "darkey" and who has designed his house to duplicate a Mississippi plantation mansion, is seen, finally, not as a person of humor but as a part of fraudulent sickness.

Tod Hackett is, at least to an extent, a self-portrait of the author, and it is West's self-knowledge that makes his novel searing and its humor both eerie and tragic.

We have been less honest than West. We have made watching atrocity and atrocity's aftermath a national pastime. We believe we can stand at the edge of the fire and speak about the gruesome taking of life, as if the scenes we see on our television are from another country, as if those on a freeway overpass cheering a celebrity accused of murder have nothing to do with ourselves.

Nathaniel West's Los Angeles is loud, evil, sexually charged and sexually degraded, violent, lurid, murderous, and celebratory of falseness. West's Hollywood was, it is clear, more than a vision of Los Angeles. Through Tod Hackett, West perceived the sickness of Los Angeles as a mirror of a national disease of senseless violence. "The Angelenos would be first [Hackett thinks], but their comrades all over the country would follow...."

However, for all of its brilliance, *Locust* is a partial vision. West, so accurate at seeing through facades of decency, has no conception of the good—everything and everyone is corrupt. In contrast, our greatest California writers have identified evil, but have celebrated characters who are brave and selfless and, even in death, not defeated.

Yet West's landscape cannot be dismissed. It is only partially true, but it is nowhere false.

Tillie Olsen's Visions of Hope

To read Tillie Olsen is to enter the world that West left out of his fiction. Olsen's four greatest stories, all collected in *Tell Me a Riddle*, delineate a world where pain, always present, is met with courage, and tragedy, when it comes, is given dimension. Olsen's characters are heroic. They argue, hurt, and disappoint one another, but because they care about each other, the stories of their lives offer the reader cleansing tears, genuine catharsis.

Three of the stories of *Tell Me a Riddle* are set in the working class Potrero Hill district of San Francisco during the 1950s. The title story takes place in the Los Angeles of elderly poor Jews, who lived in the rooms and small apartments that bordered Santa Monica 35 years ago.

Though more than a generation has passed since their publication, Olsen's stories are timeless. They contain messages that are universal. "I Stand Here Ironing" examines the relationship of mother and daughter and demonstrates how triumph can come out of deprivation. "Hey Sailor, What Ship?" is a statement about friendship, the passage of time, and the obligation we owe our fallen companions. "Oh Yes" shows us how lines of color separate us not only from each other but often from the best part of ourselves. "Tell Me a Riddle" is a tribute to an affirmation of selfhood which, Olsen shows, has a claim equal to unselfish love.

These are painful stories to read, but the emotions they touch are not emotions to be denied, and the triumphs they applaud are worth remembering.

In "I Stand Here Ironing," a life that could have ended in disaster has been saved by human resilience and courage. Helen, the mother in the story, is also the story's narrator. Helen is a character who shares much of the author's own biography and she is an important figure in all four stories, a voice and point of view that connects disparate experiences. In "I Stand Here Ironing" Helen has been deserted in Depression San Francisco and left with a young daughter, Emily, whom she has loved but has had to shunt about during childhood, depriving her of the essential protection every child deserves. Helen knows she has done her best by Emily, but also knows that Emily has been hurt. Touched by loneliness, poverty, anxiety, and loss, Emily has had a difficult time, even after Helen's remarriage. Helen tells us:

> I will never total it all... She was a child seldom smiled
> at. Her father left me before she was a year old. I had
> to work her first six years... or I sent her borne and to
> his relatives. They were years she hated... I was a young
> mother... I was a distracted mother. There were other

children pushing up, demanding…There were years she did not want me to touch her…

And yet, the essential love of the mother for her daughter has been transmitted and reciprocated. Olsen shows us that a human being is more than an accumulation of hurts. Emily, 19 years old as the story concludes (the same age Helen was when Emily was born) has more than survived; she is a college student and a performer, a comedienne who has transformed pain into art, who has become a loving daughter. Helen, watching Emily from the ironing board, reviewing her and her daughter's hard life, hopes that Emily will understand her sacrifices and thinks finally, "She is so lovely…She will find her way."

"Hey Sailor, What Ship?," on the surface the story of a sailor destroying himself through heavy drinking, is on closer reading the story of more than one man. It is a story of a San Francisco Depression generation, the men and women who were young adults during the 1934 General Strike, the idealists who fought or supported those who fought Franco in Spain, the people who found hope amid hunger and brutality and despair. The story takes place during the 1950s when Whitey, the sailor, has only one link to family life—Helen and Lennie and their children, living in a small Potrero Hill house.

Lennie and Helen cannot give Whitey up, even as he hurts them with his drinking and anger, even as he embarrasses their children. The bond of what they once were is too real to break.

To Lennie, he remained a tie to adventure and a world in which "men had not eaten each other…"

> To Helen he was the compound of much help given, much support; the ear to hear, the hand that understands how much a scrubbed floor, or a washed dish, or a child taken care of for a while, can mean….

Whitey mourns, in the privacy of his mind, the death of a dream. He thinks of the 1930s.

The City and the Fields

Understand. The death of the brotherhood. Once an
injury to one is an injury to all. Once, once they had to
live for each other...

We are left with a mother and father and children, watching a lonely
man walking in the fog down the hill away from the only home he
will ever have. We are left with parents explaining to their children the
meaning of friendship and the content of a dream, still shared.

"Oh Yes" is a story of loss. Helen and her black friend Alva arrange
to have Helen's daughter Carol invited to the baptism of Alva's daughter,
Parry. Yet what the two mothers hope will cement the children's friendship drives the girls, already facing the racial divisiveness of junior high
school, further apart. Carol faints during the church service, frightened
by the emotionality of the congregation, and Parry tells Carol she did
not want her in church at all, that she only invited her to please the
mothers. The story ends with a statement by Carol and a silent message,
in response, from Helen.

Mother, I want to forget about it all, and not care....
Why can't I forget? Oh why is it like it is and why do I
have to care?

Helen thinks:

...caring asks doing. It is a long baptism into the seas of
humankind, my daughter. Better immersion than to live
untouched...Yet how will you sustain?

"O Yes" reminds us of the difficulties of caring about others, of how
we divide ourselves racially, of how difficult yet necessary it is for us to
care.

"Tell Me a Riddle" takes the story of the all-giving and all-forgiving
Jewish mother and grandmother and stands it on its head. A woman
who has spent her life doing for others now, in her last year, dying of
cancer, refuses to cater to her often selfish husband or to her concerned

children and grandchildren. And her rage against the end of her life and the injustices of her life forces her husband and children to change, to understand a woman's sacrifices and sacredness. Helen's daughter Jeannie becomes the emotional translator between her grandmother and grandfather as her grandmother lies dying.

> That last day the agony was perpetual. Time after time it lifted her almost off the bed, so they had to fight to hold her down. He could not endure and left the room; wept as if there never would be tears enough.

> Jeannie came to comfort him. In her light voice she said, Granddaddy, Granddaddy, don't cry. She is not there, she promised me. On the last day, she said she would go back to where she first heard music. A little girl on the road of the village where she was born... it is a wedding and they dance, while the flutes so joyous and vibrant tremble in the air... Granddaddy, it is all right... Come back, come back and help her poor body to die...

And thus a grandmother's fierce assertion becomes, for grandfather and granddaughter, the occasion of final devotion. A woman's life is recognized, tragically, only as she leaves it.

Those of us who are English teachers need, I think, to help students recognize the selfless and courageous among us. But we cannot deny, in literature or in life, the world Nathaniel West painted. Every high school senior who has attended a Friday night party has seen, after midnight, scenes that are right out of *The Day of the Locust*.

It is Olsen's world to which we must aspire, for as long as we live. The young correctly are suspicious of sentimentality, but they must understand and recognize honest sentiment. They must learn the value of not giving up or giving in to despair. Tillie Olsen, herself, in an essay in *Newsweek*, January 3, 1994, said it best:

Sometimes the young—discouraged, overwhelmed—ask me incredulously: You mean you still have hope? And I hear myself saying, yes, I still have hope; beleaguered, starved, battered, based hope. Through horror, blood, betrayal, apathy, callousness, retreats, defeats—in every decade of my now 82-year-old life that hope has been tested, reaffirmed....

CHAPTER 9

World War II in California

Dorothea Lange, Toshio Mori,
Maya Angelou, Ella Leffland,
Jean Wakatsuki Houston and James Houston

Dorothea Lange: Seeking Hope

I had the good fortune while working on this book to make it to the Museum of Modern Art in San Francisco twice and view the photographs of Dorothea Lange. Lange is so like Olsen in her portraits of Depression men and women and children. Olsen's people, like Lange's, are dignified in their suffering; they are proud, unselfish, and they care for their families—despite their own deprivation.

Dorothea Lange was a literary photographer—an artist, a woman who entered California and American Literature with a moral intent and purpose. She photographed the second Gold Rush, and the San Francisco Bay Area at War (1941-1945). As historian Charles Wollenberg put it, Lange "produced a body of work that dramatically shaped America's image and understanding of the Depression." Continues Wollenberg, "When Hollywood was preparing to film John Steinbeck's *Grapes of Wrath*, director John Ford turned to Dorothea's photographs.... Her 'migrant mother,' the 1936 portrait...became one of the best-known photographs in the world and still symbolizes the Depression for millions of Americans."

Here is a photographer whose photo-essays are essays in the literary sense of the term. Her photographs are arguments on behalf of the dignity of humankind, and we believe these arguments from her evidence, from the people whose faces she captured in the midst of privation.

These people, Lange's people, are brave, compassionate, determined, undefeated.

Heyday Books' collection of Lange's work, *Photographing the Second Gold Rush,* is a pictorial document that shows us some of the people, the photographic image of those written about by John Steinbeck and William Saroyan, Toshio Mori and Hisaye Yamamoto, Maya Angelou and Tillie Olsen, and a host of other California writers. These photographs can help the reader understand California writing about the Depression and World War II and they stand, too, as works of history and art. They continue to haunt us today.

Look, for example, at the opening photograph in her book. We view a newsstand and bottle of Majestic Root Beer and Sparkling Water. We see the radio and *Popular Mechanics* magazines, and in the center we view the *San Francisco Examiner's* 6 A.M. extra, "OUSTER OF ALL JAPS IN CALIFORNIA NEAR!"

We turn the page to see a brother and sister, Japanese-American, "tagged and ready for relocation," not "Jap" aliens but frightened American children. The photo essay continues with a portrait of a proud Japanese patriarch, hat on, lost in thought, his belongings beside him, a baby granddaughter also in the photo. On the next page, we see the photograph titled "Oakland, 1942," which shows a huge sign above a storefront in Japantown, with the banner, "I AM AN AMERICAN."

Lange is the best kind of essayist, photo or word. Her details make her argument. Her argument comes out of her details.

Likewise, her photographs of the Braceros, "Mexican Workers," captures the men's dignity, strength, and fear—strangers outside of their native land.

But most of the book is composed of the photos depicting the shipyard workers that swelled the cities of Richmond and Oakland during the World War II years, when the U.S. geared to defeat Hitler and the Japanese empire.

The word that defines these men and women—Blacks and whites from Texas, Oklahoma, Arkansas, and other states devastated by the dustbowl—is purposeful. The East Bay was transformed and if racism and sexism persisted—and they did—Bay Area life was transformed for the better. Charles Wollenberg explains, in his introduction, the effect of the shipyard workers on the city of Richmond.

> A working class town of about 23,000 overwhelmingly white inhabitants in 1940, just four years later...it was a multi-ethnic city of 100,000 people...

One of Lange's greatest photographs, a photo of children was taken in Richmond. The kids, of all colors, raise their hands to indicate they have been born outside of California. Their parents' faces show, it seems to me, optimism and hope as if California, the Bay Area, is a true promised land.

We are now more than fifty years from that photograph. Where are those children—now grown? Many are now parents and grandparents themselves. Black and Chinese, Mexican and Caucasian—how many of those children's children live a life that justifies the dreams of their parents and grandparents? Surely the dream was for jobs and bread, but not for jobs and bread alone. In our time, compared to the 1930s and 1940s, a time of affluence and opportunity, how many of us have faces as noble as those photographed by Dorothea Lange?

Yet Lange's work is not depressing. She makes us aware of what is essential about life—work, direction, courage, compassion, sacrifice, justice, hope. These are emotions that must endure—and they do endure, for one of Lange's gifts is to help us see what is noble in the faces around us.

Today, on Broadway in Oakland, the scene of some of Lange's best World War II photographs, amid the 1997 crowded tableau of young gangsters and angry cops, prostitutes and pimps, businessmen and men in rags, Lange's people remain. You can see her people in the Oakland Chinatown sister holding her young brother's hand, in the Black mother in nurse's uniform waiting for a 72 bus, in the cowboy-hatted, silent Mexican smoking outside of the restaurant where he works as dishwasher, in the blonde woman paramedic helping a woman who has passed out beneath a brick apartment fire-escape. Lange, now so many years later, directs our attention to our best qualities, the qualities we need to celebrate should California survive as more than a place of gaudy dreams and false pretenses. Dorothea Lange is a literary photographer, one of California's great artists. She is an artist of the heart.

Toshio Mori Explores Japanese-American Life During WWII in *Yokohama, California*

California has given much to American literature. From Frank Norris and Jack London to John Steinbeck and William Saroyan, from Tillie Olsen and Joan Didion to Maya Angelou to Maxine Hong Kingston, California writers have helped define and universalize our national experience. In teaching American literature for these many years, I have tried to augment my book list with such California writers whose texts illustrate national themes. I want my students to understand their geography and their history within the American context. This year I will add to my list some stories of a powerful, unsung Californian and American writer, a man whose work should be more widely known. The author's name is Toshio Mori, and his poignant collection of stories is called *Yokohama, California*.

Yokohama, California includes twenty-one short stories and vignettes, prose that details the life in San Leandro, California, on the eve of, and during, World War II. Mori's collection is an achievement of both craft and spirit, for his stories illustrate brotherhood without being sentimental, make sense of tragedy without minimizing pain, stand for life without forgetting loss and death. He wrote in the face of terrible racism; he created despite the relocation and internment of the Japanese community of California and the West. And he succeeds as an author of immigrant life, joining writers like William Saroyan in his stories of Armenian-American life and Anzia Yezierska in her portrayal of Jewish-American New York.

Two of the stories in *Yokohama, California* deal directly with the pain of being Japanese-American in an age of extreme prejudice. The first is the compelling opening story, "Tomorrow Is Coming, Children," told in the voice of a grandmother addressing her grandchildren from inside a relocation camp. Mori uses the bravery of the grandmother to illustrate the patriotism and hope of a people who remained loyal Americans despite incredible mistreatment. The old woman tells her grandchildren of her feeling when she first saw America, watching the skyline of San Francisco from an immigrant ship.

> "America! America! We're in America, someone cried. Others took up the call and the deck was full of eager faces..."

The old woman has seen too much and believes in the ideals of America too strongly to give up hope. She tells her young grandchildren:

> "...time is your friend in America, children...Tomorrow is coming, children..."

A second story dealing with prejudice, "Slant-Eyed Americans," is set on the day of Pearl Harbor and ends with a Japanese-American woman telling the narrator's brother, an American soldier, "Give your best to America. Our people's honor depends on you Nisei soldiers."

Mori's work is especially relevant today when the injustice of 200,000 Americans of Japanese being interned is now finally recognized through a long-awaited reparation. In fact, "Tomorrow is Coming, Children" was first published in the Topaz relocation magazine *TRK* for a camp audience. As scholar Lawrence Inada has noted, Mori's stories are a tribute to all the brave Japanese women who "...surely [were] put into the camps, starting with the Tanforan Race track."

In essence, the stories about Japanese women are a tribute to the immigrant generation of Mori's own mother, to whose memory *Yokohama, California* is dedicated. The stories read as universal renderings of woman as mother, grandmother, and nurturer. "The Woman Who Makes Swell Doughnuts" harnesses Mori's prose into the simple poetry of the personal essay.

> There is nothing I like to do better than go to her house and knock on the door and when she opens the door

to go in. It is one of the experiences I will remember—perhaps the only immortality I will meet...in my short life...

She'd given birth to six children—worked side by side with her man for forty years. I take today to talk of her and her wonderful doughnuts when the earth is still something to her...

"My Mother Stands on Her Head" is an exploration that reveals the compassion of Mori's mother. Cheated by an unfair countryman, the mother refuses to buy from the rogue. She declares to the family that she will shop at Safeway for dairy products instead. But in the end, tolerance and community feeling allow Mori's mother to forgive the faker.

Then one day mother lost her fury, and the old habits overtook her. Ishimoto-san began coming as before...

If the women of *Yokohama, California* are drawn with quiet strength, the men are rendered with the complexity of courage, loneliness, and despair. Mori's self-portrait, "Toshio Mori," is a sketch any sensitive teenager will relate to. The fact that the story's subject is in his 20s will not bar the younger reader's understanding or identification.

Tonight he could not sit with the family and talk.

Tonight he could not listen to the radio; he could not read.

He sat, aware that no one knew him as he knew himself. He knew even Mother and his brother Hayime could not see his state of feeling...

This terrible isolation is echoed by the melancholic, boisterous drinker hero of "The End of the Line":

Sometimes I think I am going away alone. Sometimes I believe I am leaving the earth forever. Sometimes I have the feeling that I am stepping off to meet warm arms and happy greetings but that's rare.

In contrast to male isolation, Papa Noda, the hero of "Seven Children," expresses hope found through pride in family and fatherhood. Papa's hope for his children combines his feelings for his Japanese ancestry with his belief in American democracy.

I came to America to seek fame and fortune. I have found my fortune...Seven children, seven treasures. I am not famous. I work all day and I am poor. But I have seven plants, seven healthy growing plants. Maybe one a Naguchi, who knows...Lincoln or Naguchi, one man...The real man...

Among Mori's many distinctions is his ability to see life whole. *Yokohama, California* confronts the dark side of human nature. Mori sees jealousy and cruelty as the cause of war, and his understanding of how we hurt each other is profound.

Members of the 442nd must have keenly felt war as a fight of brother and brother. In three stories, "Brothers," "The Chessmen," and "Tomorrow and Today," Mori explores the underlying causes of war, exploitation and jealousy. In "Chessmen," two worthy men, a middle-aged family man and a young man on the verge of marriage, are forced to compete for the same job, and the older man is nearly destroyed physically in the process. In "Today and Tomorrow," a pretty sister, in the midst of a quarrel, badly hurts her plain sister with a cruel remark. "You are ugly, Hatsuye! You're so ugly no man will look at you."

"Brothers" takes up the cause of war through examining a fight between brothers. A five-year-old and a three-year-old fight over territory, almost killing themselves, as their father (Mori's dentist) hopelessly looks on. The father recognizes in his sons' dispute, "...that behind silence, behind little heads, their little eyes are for coveted things and their hands are to paw and smash, and the brewing trouble which is the worry and sadness of the earth is once again stirring."

But it is Mori's belief and hope that good will overcome evil and that the worthy immigrant generation's sacrifice was not made in vain. Years following Papa Noda's death, Mori comes to the Nodas' house to see George, his friend, and Papa Noda's son.

> ...In the living room I noticed Papa Noda's portrait above his desk.
>
> "That's a good portrait of him," I said to Mamoru.
>
> "It is, I wish Papa were here tonight."
>
> Later, a baby girl toddles up to Mori.
>
> "George's baby. She's Sansei, you know."
>
> "Third generation," I agreed.
>
> "Pretty soon fourth generation," she said smiling.
>
> "Shisei," I said, nodding my head and we went into the living room.

Another story, "Lil' Yokohama," integrates everyday American life with traditional family concerns. Mori moves from the excitement of two Japanese-American teams competing in a baseball game toward a hymn to tradition and to birth. "Down the block a third-generation Japanese-American is born, a boy. His father is out of town driving a truck for a grocer."

Yokohama, California is a work that lends itself to comparison and contrast with American classics. The book can easily be compared with *Red Badge of Courage*, where brothers must fight brothers; *The Crucible*, where a witch hunt threatens community; *Huckleberry Finn*, which documents the effects of racism as a disease upon our country; or *Raisin in the Sun,* which describes the strength of a family fighting racial prejudice.

California high school students need to understand how our region reflects the national literature and how the themes expressed by California writers are national themes. Now, because of Mori, one can see San Leandro, and all the West Coast Yokohamas, as immigrant places, where old people remember the trials of becoming American, and where life is celebrated, but not at the cost of forgetting cruelty and prejudice.

Maya Angelou: A Caged Bird in San Francisco

> There is a true yearning to respond to
> The singing River and the wise Rock.
> So say the Asian, the Hispanic, the Jew
> The African and Native American, the Sioux
> The Catholic, the Muslim, the French, the Greek
> The Irish, the Rabbi, the Priest...

Maya Angelou's Inaugural Poem reinforces the ideal of America as a place of many cultures, a nation of nations, that could be, if only we recognize ourselves as brothers and sisters, a place of hope.

Angelou is an American artist, an internationalist, an African-American, a Southerner in her earliest years, a feminist. She is also an important California writer. *I Know Why the Caged Bird Sings,* the first volume of her autobiography, moves from Stamps, Arkansas, to the Oakland and San Francisco of the World War II years. Her rendering of her time in the Bay Area concludes *Caged Bird* and adds another important chapter to California literature.

Angelou arrived in California at the crossroads year of 1941, when poor Blacks and Southern whites met California's Asian, Hispanic, and white ethnic communities. She arrived as California was becoming truly an American place, haven to the oppressed from America and the world, but a haven marred by prejudice and hatreds, some imported, some homegrown.

Caged Bird is an autobiography that has the feel of a strong novel.

Maya—Marguerite—is her own central character, and Angelou paints the pictures of her grandmother, her proud handicapped uncle, her wild yet protective brother, and her hometown of Stamps with real artistry and close appreciation of the terrors and longings of childhood. The evils of segregation are revealed in a chilling graduation sequence when Angelou's eighth grade class is patronized and demeaned by a white educator and guest speaker who seems unaware, even, of the damage he has wrought. But the Blacks of Stamps are undefeated and we see, in Angelou's narration and descriptions, the seeds of courage that would later fuel the Civil Rights movement.

The author remembers Oakland and San Francisco as she encountered them at the age of 13, a shy, gawky girl who had suffered from both the white racism of the South and from a devastating rape at the hands of a black man. The girl and her brother, Baily, come to California to join their mother, who had left the children with her mother-in-law, in effect abandoning them, years before.

Angelou, in *Caged Bird,* will define Afro-American courage, but she is not hesitant, beginning with the story of her rape, to paint her people's experience in its full human dimension, including its cruelty and its harshness. Sensitivity was, in the community, often considered a weakness. Here, Angelou describes her mother:

> With all her jollity, Vivian Baxter had no mercy. There was a saying at the time, which if she didn't say it herself, explained her attitude. The saying was, "Sympathy is next to shit in the dictionary and I can't even read…"

When the family moves to San Francisco, Angelou notes the historical facts that brought Blacks to the Western Addition, to replace Japanese-Americans who had their property stolen from them and who were forced into relocation camps. Angelou, in her honesty, notes that the newcomers gave little thought to the fellow victims of oppression they had replaced.

> …The Japanese shops which sold products to Nisei customers were taken over by enterprising Negro business-

men and in less than a year became permanent homes for Southern Blacks...

> For the first time he could think of himself as a Boss, a Spender. He was able to pay other people to work for him...Who could expect this man to share his new and dizzying importance with concern for a race he had never known to exist?

Angelou is, at first, enthralled by The City, and a freedom she had never experienced: "...I became dauntless and free of fears, intoxicated by the physical fact of San Francisco...I was certain no one loved her as impartially as I..." But San Francisco was becoming another Northern American city, a place more and more like Chicago, Detroit, New York, and Philadelphia, a place of hope, but a place that often replayed traditional conflicts of whites and Blacks.

> Southern white illiterates brought their biases intact to the West from the hills of Arkansas and the swamps of Georgia...The Black ex-farmers had not lost their distrust of whites...

War-time sacrifice by Black soldiers made racism against African-Americans especially repugnant. Angelou tells a story, popular in Black San Francisco during the war years, of a white matron who refuses to sit next to a Negro on a streetcar. She is angry because the Black is out of uniform while her son is fighting on Iwo Jima.

> The story said that the man pulled his body away from the window to show an armless sleeve. He said quietly and with great dignity, "Then ask your son to look around for my arm which I left over there..."

Despite the existence of prejudice, Marguerite experiences San Francisco as a deliverance from the segregated South. She succeeds in school, is respected by teachers and fellow students of all races, and lies about her age to become, remarkably, the first Black streetcar conductor in the history of San Francisco. Yet her ascent seems ended when, after her first experiment with sex, she becomes pregnant by a neighborhood boy whom she does not really care for.

What might have been a tragedy instead provides the autobiography with an ending of beauty and reconciliation. Maya's tough, no-nonsense mother offers her daughter—finally—acceptance, sympathy, and protection. Vivian, the mother of no mercy, has followed her heart, and so forever grandmother, daughter, and grandson have been linked by bonds of love. Marguerite's mother has softened, changed; she reassured Marguerite about her new son.

> ...I found that I was lying on my stomach with my arm bent at a right angle. Under the tent of blanket, which was poled by my elbow and forearm, the baby slept touching at my side.

> Mother whispered, "See you don't have to think about doing the right thing...(When) you're for the right thing, then you do it without thinking..."

Angelou is a writer of empathy and hope. She argues, in *Caged Bird*, that we can, as individuals, change, become more compassionate, use our time on earth to redeem instead of oppress.

It has been now over twenty years since the Rodney King riots when innocent people, from every race, lost their lives, murdered.

Too many of us have chosen to define ourselves in the most narrow racial ethnic sense. We do not know each other. Vicious stereotypes abound—about Koreans and other Asian-Americans, Blacks, Caucasians, Hispanics. Exaggeration is the name of the game. We have lost our sense of sympathy, and sympathy, as Angelou shows in *Caged Bird*, is not easily achieved, just as compassion must be demonstrated to become real.

The language of the conservative suburb, the politically correct classroom, and the streets has been divisive, simplistic, and self-serving.

Angelou's work will not please haters. She was moving, in *Caged Bird*, through painful tests of loneliness, isolation, and abuse—towards the reconciliation and affirmations of her inaugural poem, a poem totally appropriate to the national and California condition. We can do better. We do not have to hate and fear and hurt each other.

> Here on the pulse of this new day
> You may have the grace to look up and out
> And into your sister's eyes, into
> Your brother's face, your country
> And say simply
> With hope
> Good morning.

Ella Leffland and Jean Wakatsuki: Images from World War II

"I thought the opposite shore was Denmark, the place my parents came from. Then I learned that it was only Benicia, a town like our own, and my brother showed me where Denmark was on his world map. I remembered it as a purple dot on the other side of an immense ocean."

—*Ella Leffland*, Rumors of Peace

"We were alone out there, too far from the road to hear anything but wind. I thought of Mama, now seven years gone. For a long time I stood gazing at the monument. I couldn't step inside the fence. I believe in ghosts and spirits. I knew I was in the presence of those who had died at Manzanar..."

—*Jean Wakatsuki*, Farewell to Manzanar

During World War II, nearly 300,000 Americans fell in battle, 115,000 others died in service-related deaths, and 670,856, according to *The World Almanac*, suffered wounds that were not mortal. In Europe, more than 6,000,000 Jewish people and millions of others perished in Nazi concentration camps. The Germans murdered civilian populations and bombed cities like Rotterdam, which had already surrendered. Hitler's ally, Japan, committed war crimes and atrocities against the population of China and the Philippines, and, contrary to the Geneva conventions, tortured Allied prisoners of war.

Meanwhile, in the United States, Japanese-Americans were interned in relocation camps. This, despite the fact that, as historian Henry Steele Commager would write in 1947, "...the record doesn't disclose a single case of sabotage during the whole war...," or that of the 110,000 interred on the west coast, Japanese-American men volunteered in high numbers, and the 442nd all-Japanese battalion became the most decorated American combat unit of the war.

How much do our high school and even college students know about World War II? Many of our students, polls have shown, know little about the Holocaust, let alone the internment of the Japanese or the historic beginnings of World War II. Twenty-five percent, according to a 1988 ABC poll, do not even know that the Japanese bombing of Pearl Harbor brought us into the war. Now, nearly 50 years after the war's end, many young people regard World War II as ancient history.

Two California works—Ella Leffland's novel *Rumors of Peace* and Jean Wakatsuki Houston and James Houston's *Farewell to Manzanar*—both bring to life the California of 1941–1945. Both works allow us to view the past through the eyes of young girls growing toward womanhood. These are literary works that have the ability to teach history and the power to make the past real.

Ella Leffland: *Rumors of Peace*

Ella Leffland's *Rumors of Peace* is a coming-of-age story. The novel's heroine, Suse (pronounced "souza"), daughter of Danish immigrants, is ten years old when Pearl Harbor was attacked, and the war, as viewed from Mendoza (in real life Martinez, thirty miles east of San Francisco on the Carquinez Strait and a few miles from the Port Chicago Naval Station) provides the context and setting of the novel. The narrator grows up during those four years of war and changes from a frightened, hysterical child into a person on the verge of womanhood, involved with a portion of the world's suffering.

Leffland shows the war as disruption. Suse's own formerly close-knit family breaks up. Her sister, a high school senior when the novel opens, moves to Los Angeles; her brother, Peter, is drafted and takes part in the Battle of the Bulge. Suse's father relocates his work to Oakland and Suse, sensitive but not a model child, is left with friends and peers—including the intellectual, eccentric older sister of a schoolmate—to search for the meaning of what she intuitively and correctly identifies as tragedy.

Suse herself is a realistic character, in that she is presented as both kind and capable of cruelty, sympathetic to the suffering in Europe, yet cruelly unsympathetic to the suffering of the Japanese-Americans of her hometown. Leffland shows the effect of racial prejudice on a young girl. Though Suse's parents are sympathetic to the pain of the Japanese-Americans, Suse is not, and she is encouraged in her bigotry, Leffland shows, by the influential in society. The narrator remembers:

> Even important people understood, because I now read the San Francisco papers when I was at the library and ran my finger under statements by governors, generals and famous columnists...

Suse quotes a well-known columnist:

> Why treat the Japs well here? They take the parking positions. They get ahead of you at the stamp line at the post office. Let 'em be pinched, hurt, hungry and dead up against it. Personally, I hate the Japanese and that goes for all of them.

Even as Suse grows up and understands, or at least begins to understand, the irrationality of her feelings toward Japanese-Americans, she states, "they were people I would never be able to give a spontaneous smile..." Here, it is obvious, that Leffland is not speaking for herself but is, instead, showing us the way propaganda poisons, years after the fact.

It is ironic that Suse, so sympathetic to the suffering of the victims of the Nazis, should not see other victims, close to home, but here, again, Suse is rendered as a realistic, flawed, human creation.

Leffland brings us many memorable passages. One scene especially, the death of President Roosevelt, as experienced on a junior high school afternoon, reminded me, in its poignancy, of the afternoon, when I was in junior high school, when we learned of President Kennedy's death.

Finally, one is left with Leffland's narrator, and her insightful and sympathetic understanding of how her life has been changed by the war. Whatever her limitation, Suse has perceived a part of the world outside of herself. She remembers an Italian-American grocery boy from her hometown who has died in the war, and his death allows her to reflect upon the death of other innocents.

> And then a strange picture came to me...and the people in the bombed cellars of London and Rotterdam, the soldiers lying dead in the snow and their arms sticking up like iron, and in the jungles, rotting...they had all been real inside, important. Frank Garibaldi in his green apron, coming up the steps, whistling his complicated tunes...he must have hated to die. He must have cried and covered his eyes...and why should I have to see such a thing now, just when I knew we were safe...

Ella Leffland, through her novel, imparts to us the knowledge that no one alive during the years of World War II could escape living with the consequences of tragic history.

Jean Wakatsuki and James Houston: *Farewell to Manzanar*

Jean Wakatsuki Houston's memoir, written with her husband, acclaimed novelist James Houston, is a small masterpiece and takes over where *Rumors of Peace* leaves off. Unlike Suse, Jean was one of the war's true victims. She was only eight years old, living in Long Beach, the youngest of nine children of a loving mother and a brilliant, talented, mercurial fisherman father when Pearl Harbor was bombed and her world caved in.

For Jean Wakatsuki, unlike Suse, nothing is abstract. Everything in *Farewell to Manzanar* is painfully real. And unlike Leffland's heroine, Jean has no time for dreaming.

Manzanar, as the Houstons make clear, was not a Nazi extermination camp, but the humiliations of Manzanar were real and cannot be erased. Jean takes us through an episode of indignity of restroom sewage and water overflowing, and the humiliation of the female elders having to go to the restrooms without stalls—and so improvising cardboard separations.

Worse was the accusation of disloyalty. In a preface, the Houstons trace the history of anti-Japanese and anti-Asian prejudice and make the undeniable point that it was the Japanese-Americans and not the German-Americans who were interred, an illustration of racial prejudice. Japanese-Americans, though betrayed by the United States, remained loyal to this country; and the Japanese revolt at Manzanar, short lived, came not because of disloyalty, Jean Wakatsuki makes clear, but because of maltreatment, poor living conditions, and the belief that "...the camp's chief steward, a Caucasian, [had] stolen sugar... to sell on the black market. Since it was rumored that infants had died from saccharin mixed into formulas as a sugar substitute, these charges were widely believed..."

The young generation—the Nisei—born in America have been hurt but not crippled by the internment. It is the Issei, the generation of Jean's father—born in Japan—that have been nearly ruined. The elders, who are loyal to America, but who remember Japan, will not forget their cruel treatment.

Jean's father, after Pearl Harbor, has suffered in federal prison. It will be a year until he joins the family at Manzanar, cleared of the charge of treason. He has been honest during an F.B.I. interrogation and therefore has been under suspicion as a spy. "I feel sorry for both countries," he has stated. Mr. Wakatsuki explains to the F.B.I. man,

> "...The Japanese are courageous fighters, and they will fight well. But their leaders are stupid. I weep every

night for my country...[I] have lived in this country nine years longer than you have, do you realize that? Yet I am prevented by law from owning land. I am now separated from my family without cause...

Jean's father, when he is reunited with his family at Manzanar, is a nearly totally embittered man.

Jean has, too, been forever marked. Every racial incident, every racial comment, following the years of internment, brings back the experience of non-acceptance. During the remaining years at Manzanar, Jean's father has become a violent alcoholic. Finally, after the war, he stops drinking and moves the family to Santa Clara, where even Jean's election as homecoming queen cannot quell his suspicion and anger. Nor can Jean's election end her own feeling of being trapped, forever, between two worlds.

Houston's conclusion is eloquent in the legacy of the internment. It is 1972:

I heard Mama's soft weary voice from 1945 say, It's starting over, I knew it wouldn't. Yet neither would I be surprised to find the FBI at the door again...Manzanar would always live in my nervous system, a needle with Mama's voice....

Final Thoughts

It would be nice to think that after World War II, after the gas chambers, after the defeat of an Axis of absolute racism and evil, that the world, including we in America, would leave prejudice behind.

But we know that the world, forever changed, was not born again in 1945, but continued. When Jean Wakatsuki stands at Manzanar and pays homage to the memory of her mother and her father, one finds the continuity that gives hope. That she stands with her Caucasian husband and their children gives special hope. Leffland's novel reminds us of the stakes of the Second World War—that America fought an empire of pure evil and that the world would have been lost forever had we been defeated. The Houstons' book reminds us that fighting pure evil did not make us pure good.

Those of us born in the decade and a half after World War II are the links between our parents who lived through the Depression and World War and our students, who were born after JFK, Robert Kennedy, and Martin Luther King, Jr. As teachers, we can introduce our students to the pain and turmoil and triumphs of the world of their grandparents. Our students need to understand that their time, for all of its horrors, is not unique in its difficulties. Students, understanding the painful passages of other generations, might learn to face their own time of growing up with courage instead of anger or brutality or despair.

CHAPTER 10

Latino Voices, World War II and the 1950s

Jose Villareal, Floyd Salas and Luis Valdez

Those readers who have become cognizant of the explosive growth of Latino-American writing, who have read Rudolfo Anaya, Piri Thomas, Judith Ortiz-Cofer, Sandra Cisneros, Julia Alvarez, Gary Soto, Richard Rodriguez and Luis Rodriguez, among many others—are aware that Hispanic-American literature has taken its place as an important piece of American literature. Two of the first wave of Hispanic-American writers were Californians.

They are Jose Antonio Villareal, author of the 1959 novel *Pocho*, the first novel by a Mexican-American born of Mexican-immigrant parents, and Floyd Salas, novelist, poet and essayist, whose Joseph Henry Jackson-award-winning *Tattoo the Wicked Cross* is a classic of American prison literature and whose 1992 memoir, *Buffalo Nickel*, is a portrait of Oakland during World War II and after.

Both Villareal and Salas began publishing before the advent of the Chicano movement and write more as individuals than as representatives of race. In fact, the Chicano movement had little effect on their subsequent work, for both men are rebels who would always go their own way. Through their work is illuminated a piece of World War II era multi-ethnic California. The rediscovery of writers like Salas and Villareal is a good sign. To quote novelist and critic Ilan Stavans, "When some new ethnic writers become national treasures it will be in part because of the generation of Salas, Anaya, Thomas…as their compass."

A third Latino writer, only a decade or so younger, but of another generation, the acclaimed playwright Luis Valdez, born in 1940, also wrote of Latino World War II California in his play, *Zoot Suit*, which I will discuss in the conclusion of this essay alongside his classic *La Bamba*. Valdez is the bridge between Villareal and Salas and the younger veterans of the Chicano movement like Luis Rodriguez. *Pocho* and *Buffalo Nickel* are front-line reports from the World War II era. *Zoot Suit* is less a report than an interpretation. These works together provide some essential background to the issues facing Latinos in California today.

Jose Villareal

"The watershed event in the development of the Latino coming of age story was the 1959 publication of Jose Antonio Villareal's novel *Pocho*…"

—*Ilan Stavans*

Pocho opens in Juarez during the Mexican revolution and moves to the Santa Clara Valley of the Depression and World War II. The novel is unique in the strength of its characters, settings and themes. The main character and central viewpoint of the novel is that of Richard. But the novel begins with Richard's father, Juan, and tells the story of Juan's movement, from being a brave soldier who rode with Villa, to his life as the father of a large family in the Santa Clara Valley.

Mr. Rubio dreams of Mexico in the way religious Jews yearn for Israel, repeating, "…next year we will have enough money. Next year, next year." But there will be no return to Mexico and the novel's most intense focus narrows to the trinity of father, mother and son.

The Rubio family, though they settle in Santa Clara, rich valley farm land, forty miles south of San Francisco are uprooted individuals, and Juan Rubio becomes unhappy when his wife Consuelo's new-found freedom in America destroys his conception of marriage. When Consuelo can no longer forgive Mr. Rubio's infidelities or tolerate his physical abuse, Richard is caught between two powerful parents, who love him, but whose expectations for him are impossible for him to fulfill.

Despite Richard's friendships with children of other ethnicities—Portuguese, Spanish, Italian, and Japanese—as well as fellow Mexican-Americans who have come north from Los Angeles, Richard is alienated from his place of growing up. The dreams of his friends are not his dreams. Villareal shows Richard's alienation as a function of sensitivity and intelligence. Villareal's hero is unusual in that he does not give in to parental or peer pressure. Villareal sharply contrasts Richard with the young "pachucos" and "Zoot Suiters" who settle in Santa Clara during World War II.

The "pachucos," writes Villareal, "attempted to segregate themselves from both their cultures (American and Mexican) and they became a truly lost race..." Though Richard makes friends with the pachucos and sympathizes with their anger at discrimination, he is critical of them.

> ...They had a burning contempt for people of different ancestry, whom they called Americans, and a marked hauteur towards Mexico and towards their parents for their old-country ways...

Here, Villareal's differences with militant Chicano nationalists like Luis Rodriguez, author of the acclaimed *Always Running*, could not be more clear. Unlike today's political activists, the earliest Mexican-American novelists believed in individual, not group salvation. Villareal writes:

> ...Richard understood them and partly sympathized but their way of life was not entirely justified in his mind, for he felt that they were somehow reneging on life. This was the easiest thing for them to do...

At the novel's conclusion, Richard has graduated high school, has worked full time to help support his large family, and has decided to eventually not only go to college but to become a writer. But it is World War II and he has joined the Navy as a way of leaving Santa Clara forever. His parents' marriage is over, which devastates his mother, and his father has found a rebirth of dignity with a new woman.

Richard Rubio is a young man leaving his hometown of Santa Clara much as Sherwood Anderson's George Willard left Winesburg, Ohio, not as an innocent in pursuit of ephemeral happiness but as a young man in search of dignity and a way to express, through art, the life he has known. Experience, loss of innocence, has not destroyed him. Writes Villareal:

> He thought of all the beautiful people he had known, of his father and mother in another time...of what worth was it all? His father had won his battle. But what about me? thought Richard. He would strive to live. He knew he would never be coming back...

Pocho is dedicated, in Spanish, to Villareal's father and to the memory of his mother and it is Richard's father who best articulates the novel's conception of what it means to be a Mexican-American in California. For Villareal, the personal is more important than the political. To be Mexican is not, Richard thinks, about Aztec sacrifices or gang oaths or about percentage of Indian and Spanish blood. It is, as Juan Rubio states to his son, to

> "never let anything stand in your way...promise me that you will be true unto yourself, unto what you honestly believe is right. And...do not ever forget you are Mexican..."

Here Villareal anticipates Richard Rodriguez in Rodriguez' belief that Mexico's contribution to California is the ability to find dignity and laughter in a life so brief and so often filled with pain. *Pocho*'s portraits are memorable and enrich California literature, for Juan Rubio, Consuelo and Richard are suffering but not lost. They are dignified Mexican-Americans who love one another and who struggle to be true to themselves.

Floyd Salas: *Buffalo Nickel*

One of the strongest passages of Floyd Salas' powerful *Buffalo Nickel* occurs when Salas' brother Eddie returns home from the Navy to find 13-year-old Floyd dresses as a Zoot Suiter in imitation of a pachuco.

The Salas family has moved from Denver, Colorado, to Shasta, California, and finally to Oakland. It is World War II and Floyd's mother has died and Floyd's father is drinking heavily, emotionally adrift. Floyd is being pulled in different directions by two men—two older brothers— Al, a prizefighter, drinker, and con-man who has taught Floyd to box, but has lied his way out of the military, is embarked on the way toward a path of heroin addiction and thievery. Floyd's other older brother, Eddie, is on the other hand, a troubled, talented, and brilliant idealist who has volunteered for combat.

Floyd is eating dinner alone when Eddie, on leave, surprises Floyd at home:

> "Floyd! I didn't recognize you."

> ...The next day when I came home from school in my Levis, I found that he'd [Eddie] taken scissors and cut my gabardine drapes into shreds. He held them up so I could see them. "This is what I think of your zoot suit pants," he said.

> "You can't go around looking like some lower class thug, Floyd," he said. "What would mother think?"

Eddie's focus is to engage Floyd in school and with learning and Floyd begins, under Eddie's influence, to lose some of his admiration for Al.

> ...Al was always talking about what a sissy Eddie was as a boy, when he got the highest G.P.A. in his graduating class in Denver. Since Al had come back from the

Army, I'd absorbed his likes and dislikes and rebellious attitudes towards Dad...

Buffalo Nickel deals with some very painful memories, from the death of Salas' mother to a succession of deaths of Al's heroin-addicted children. But the core of the autobiography for me is Floyd's choice of which brother to emulate, of how to become a man. It is to Salas' credit that he follows the less flashy Eddie.

Eddie has been a Naval officer and becomes, after World War II, a pharmacist in San Francisco as well as a published writer. In a strong passage, Floyd tries to comfort Eddie, who is depressed over his mother's death and his father's lack of respect for him, and the bisexuality that he thinks makes him less a man.

Floyd tries, in this exchange, to console his older brother.

> "Even if you're not a pro boxer like Al, or had a couple of amateur fights like me, you've been a Naval officer in wartime and have been decorated for it. You're more of a man than either Al or me because you've done more in a man's world."

> "Not to Dad."

Floyd cannot save Eddie from suicide, but Eddie, in death, serves as Floyd's model in Floyd's choice of becoming a writer and political idealist. For Salas is an Hispanic writer and, too, a man of the left—whose ideas are universalist, concerned with the betterment of humankind. Like Villareal, being a writer, for Salas, is a way of confronting an often-tragic world. Gerald Haslam has described Salas best:

> He is indeed a hard man, unafraid and willing—physically if necessary—to confront adversaries, but he is also sensitive, capable of great empathy and love...

Luis Valdez: *Zoot Suit* and *La Bamba*

Zoot Suit is based upon two real cases, the Sleepy Lagoon and the Zoot Suit murders but is less about historical fact than about the myth of the pachucos, which Valdez transforms into a symbolic, universal celebration of Latino courage. The play, despite its Chicano focus, is truly multicultural and the introduction of the Jewish woman attorney and her discussion of the Nazis makes the strong point that it is world-wide prejudice that is the enemy and that should unite all oppressed groups. Valdez, creator of Teatro Campasino, idolized Cesar Chavez and has stated that Chavez, the man of nonviolence, embodies the true attributes of what it means to be a hero. *Zoot Suit,* however, sympathizes with the pachucos, and makes the point that these men were far more than gangsters.

Artistically, I prefer Valdez's screenplay, *La Bamba,* where Valdez's rendering of true-life rock star Ritchie Valens and his brother, Bob, communicate across all racial categories. In *La Bamba* the pachuco and the gentle Latino rocker are on some level incomplete without the other; where American pride and Mexican honor come together in the story of an extraordinary young man, fiercer than he ever seemed, dead way too soon.

The story of Ritchie battling "a world I never made" through his music eventually finds a counterpoint in Bob's choice not to be a gangster but a responsible father who takes care of his daughter. Bob's decision brought me back to *Pocho* and Villareal's injunction to never forget being Mexican, and to always try to do what is right.

La Bamba was a film, like the later *Joy Luck Club* that instilled ethnic pride without running from the acknowledgment of ethnic cruelty. Valdez wrote about a man and a culture to make the universal argument for talent and passion as opposed to criminality. Valdez's Valens is an American and Mexican hero.

Villareal, Salas, and Valdez have individualized the Latino experience. They have given Latino writers in California at the end of the 20th century a place to stand. They have done so with pride and honesty, celebrating courage but not forgetting that part of their experience embroiled with loss, contradiction, and pain.

PART IV

From the 1950s
to the 1980s

(from top left, clockwise) Cover of News
from Native California *(courtesy of* News
from Native California *magazine; photo
courtesy of Kathleen Smith), Black Panthers
button, Haight-Ashbury, Gary Soto, Jack
Kerouac signature, Maxine Hong Kingston,
from the* Fat City *movie poster*

CHAPTER 11

Chinese Men and Woman Warriors

Frank Chin, Maxine Hong Kingston and Gus Lee

Frank Chin and *The Big Aiieee*

The anthology of Chinese-American and Japanese-American litera-ture called *The Big Aiieee* opens with a 92-page essay by playwright, short story writer, and co-editor Frank Chin. Chin's essay is, among other things, an attack upon the most well known of Chinese-American writers—Amy Tan, Maxine Hong Kingston, Jade Snow Wong, and Da-vid Henry Hwang.

Chin's essay is angry, provocative, and well-written, and the anthol-ogy deserves a reading from anyone interested in Asian-American, Cali-fornia, or West Coast writing.

I disagree with Chin's conclusion regarding the most famous of Chinese-American writers. But I do believe that Chin's essay raises important, even crucial questions about the way we read both ethnic and regional American writing.

As an American Jew, I am aware that for many readers I.B. Singer became the only Yiddish immigrant writer, and therefore scores of important poets and prose writers who wrote realistically of European and immigrant American life never found the audience they deserved. Likewise, I recall how the stereotypes in Philip Roth's *Portnoy's Complaint* became accepted by too many non-Jews and Jews as some kind of gospel truth about the Jewish mother and Jewish family.

In regional writing, William Faulkner has become *The South;* Nathan-iel Hawthorne, *New England;* John Steinbeck, *California;* and Saul Bel-low, *Chicago.* Great as these writers are, it is too simple to think of a single or two or three writers as representing an entire region or people.

In the case of Hong Kingston, Amy Tan, and Snow, Chin argues that their image of Chinese-America—especially Chinese-American men—is incomplete and inaccurate. Whether Chin is wrong or right about these three writers is less important than his argument and scholarship, which democratizes literature and calls out for a response.

An essay like Chin's is not only a comment upon literature, it is a part of literature itself. And California writing, if it is to be vital, should be read and responded to. The health of ethnic and regional writing depends upon response. And here, Chin responds with a vengeance.

Here are three of Chin's main arguments:

(1) Chin feels that too much of Chinese-American writing lies and perpetuates stereotypes about Chinese men. For this, he blames not only the majority culture but also fellow Asian-American writers and artists.

Writes Chin:

> Beulah Quo served as historical consultant in the making of the two-part "China Doll" episode of ABC TV's *How the West Was Won*. She and other AAPPA members—among them Robert Ito, Kery Ceite, James Hong, and Rosalind Chin filled the large and small roles of Chinese characters.

> Quo and the AAPPA encouraged producer John Mantley to exploit the stereotype of despicable men and victim women found in Kingston's *Woman Warrior* and Hwang's FOB and to create a brand new vicious stereotype for the Chinese to live down. Three times "Chinese say" and three times "China Doll" shows Chinese men selling Chinese women naked and in chains, in the streets of S.F.'s Chinatown. Chinese men never sold Chinese women, either naked or in Chinatown. Never. The most rabid and imaginative race-baiting whites out in the streets of the time never saw it; not even in their

nightmare fiction of foul heathens wiping out the white race with all manners of moral persuasion did they dream of Chinese men selling women chained up and naked on the streets...

(2) Chin believes that the immigrant generation has been slandered by prominent Chinese-American authors. In particular, it is his opinion that the Tongs have not been understood. Here he quotes from the bylaws of the Lung King Tin Yee Association, U.S.A. to make his point. From the bylaws:

> "...The objective and purpose being that the heritage of loyalty, fraternity, and solidarity of the Four names shall enhance the spirit of cooperation of the families and promote general welfare."

Chin writes:

> The Lung Fong Association, like all tongs, appeared in China only after it had been established in America. Tongs themselves are examples of the new art born of new experiences and informed by the heroic tradition in Asian Childhood literature and myth.

(3) Chin argues that Maxine Hong Kingston and other writers have falsified Chinese myths and legends and twisted the heroic tradition of Confucian story into one that denigrates women. He quotes Maxine Hong Kingston to prove his point. Maxine Hong Kingston has stated:

> "I'm not even saying that those are myths anymore. I'm saying I've written down American myths. Fa Mulan and the writing on her back is an American myth and I made it that way."

Chin responds in anger:

...No offense was taken at characterizing Chinese fairy tales and children's literature of the heroic tradition as teaching both contempt for women and wife beating. Clearly, Chinese-American writing by Christian auto-biographers has had the effect of displacing history with stereotype...

To sum up: Chin's arguments are explosive in their statements and *Aiieee* is a treasury of Japanese and Chinese-American literature. Chin's essay reminds us that in our desire to find what is universal in literature, we should not overlook the true facts of an ethnic or regional life. Chin's essay reveals the diversity within Asian-California writing. Asian-American writers do not speak with a single voice, and Chin's voice is one of the voices that deserve to be heard and considered.

Maxine Hong Kingston: *The Woman Warrior*

Maxine Hong Kingston's *The Woman Warrior* is a biography, the 1976 winner of the National Book Critics Circle Award and the first of three narrations that have won for the author national and international recognition. Where Chin's desire is to explore historic realities, Hong Kingston is a creative writer who, as she says, has created her own Chinese-American mythology. Her intent, it seems to me, is personal; she is writing out of a desire to understand not a whole culture but a single person—her immigrant mother. Her mother's stories may not be factual. They are told as part of a mother and daughter's acculturation into America. Maxine Hong Kingston's mother is rendered as a series of portraits. Her daughter shows us a woman who has lost two children in China, who, a doctor in China, cannot practice medicine in the United States, whose family has suffered first during the Japanese occupation during World War II and then after during the Communist takeover. All these traumas find focus in Stockton's Chinatown during the years after World War II and the daughter/storyteller thus must come to terms with a mother's endless pain and intolerable expectations. Maxine's creation of a personal mythology reads, at least to me, like universal daydreams of revenge and escape. Here, Kingston could be an African-American girl whose mother survived Southern lynchings and segregation or a Jewish daughter of Holocaust survivors or a Japanese-American girl listening to stories of internment.

The writer can perceive only her mother's suffering and her mother's rage. To be a woman warrior is to find a way out, to avenge a mother's suffering and to transcend a mother's pain. Maxine dreams of becoming a hero for her mother, for her people. But her reality is a mother who tells stories about an aunt who commits suicide rather than be shamed for a pregnancy by a man not her husband. Maxine's reality, too, is her uncle who rewards his boy nephews with "candy and new toys" but "when he heard girls' voices he turned on us and roared, 'No girls!'"

Hong Kingston writes out of anger of being overlooked and rejected.

> When they walked through Chinatown, the people must have said, "A boy—and another boy—and another boy!..."

She writes in real anger.

> At my great-uncle's funeral I secretly tested out feeling glad that he was dead—the six foot bearish...him.

Frank Chin is, I feel, wrong however, about the reasons for the appeal of this book and Hong Kingston and Tan's general appeal. Maxine Hong Kingston articulated, through her own story, the anger of a whole generation of American women, of all races and religions, who believe they have been victimized by a "patriarchal" culture. This audience does not care about the actual reality of Confucian religion. Hong Kingston's anger struck a chord with women who wanted, and accomplished, a break with familial traditions. This is a book of one who came of age during the 1960s; this is the autobiography of an American woman.

> I went away to college—Berkeley in the sixties—and I studied, and marched to change the world but I did not

turn into a boy. I would have liked to bring myself back as a boy for my parents to welcome with chickens and pigs. That was for my brother, who retuned alive from Vietnam.

But the book is not an angry book only. For Maxine Hong Kingston also writes about reconciliation, with parents and with her heritage. Far from being ashamed of being Chinese, her book transforms her into a woman warrior—a person heroic for her people and a woman respected by her mother. These daydreams or myths lead the real-life Maxine to assert herself with her mother and to gain from her mother at least a truce and an admission of a mother's love. Is it too sentimental to believe, at book's end, that the mother is proud of the assertive, capable, talented woman she helped to create?

And in the later novel *Tripmaster Monkey,* Maxine Hong Kingston's Chinese male hero defies the Chinese male stereotype. It is as if Maxine Hong Kingston had not only read Frank Chin but as if she had responded to his criticism with a creation that Chin, himself, could respect.

Gus Lee: *China Boy*

China Boy is about combat of a straightforward kind. Gus Lee's novel is about a young Chinese boy who battles, literally, for his life on the streets. The boy's life is formed by a most major tragedy, the death of his loving Chinese immigrant mother, who had protected him—and the arrival of a white stepmother who treats the boy and his sister in the cruelest possible manner—including beatings and emotional degradations. In this novel, in the form of a first person narrative, we see the life on the streets of the San Francisco Panhandle, that strip of neighborhood bordered by Golden Gate Park and Haight Street and the Fillmore, where blacks from the South met refugees from China, the rest of America and the world. Lee writes, through his narrator, Kai Ting:

> When I arrived squalling—no doubt prescient about
> my imminent fate—the street was half black. By the

time I was in the second grade and in the center of the frying pan, I was the only Asian, the only non-black and the only certified no-question-about-it-non-fighter in the district...

Gus Lee connects the Chinese and Blacks as fellow immigrant groups. But when Kai's mother dies when the boy is five, his life becomes a nightmare of being preyed upon by thugs in school and on the street.

The novel's power comes through Kai not accepting his fate and through the arrival of sympathetic characters, who Kai meets at the YMCA, men who teach Kai to box and to stand up for himself physically and who offer the boy, too, protection and love. Lee portrays a group of caring men and women and, by so doing, recreates the San Francisco of the early 1950s as a great city, great through the heroic quality of its people. The people include the Black mother of Toussaint, Kai's first friend; an Italian former pro boxer; a Mexican-American garage mechanic; and Kai's uncle. These people link two heroic traditions, the Chinese and the American, and when Kai proves himself through combat by beating up the worst Panhandle bully, we are moved because we know how close the boy has been to total destruction. Lee has recreated a real city with real people. The ending is realistic as well as triumphant. Kai is a model for children who, despite pain, do not give up. Lee's novel is in the California tradition of Jack London conquering poverty, of William Saroyan, learning to live with the loss by death of a parent. Lee is an important California writer.

Conclusion

Finally, I would like to recommend *Long Time California: A Documentary Study of an American Chinatown* by Victor G. and Brett Nee. The oral history is divided into a series of interview chapters with titles such as "Bachelor Society," "The Refugees," "Working Class," and "Radicals of a New Vision." Among many others, an interview with Frank Chin is part of the book.

My essay is, by its very nature, not complete. Chinese California has already produced some major California and American authors and a body of lesser-known but talented writers. If Chinese California has specific characters and settings, its themes are universal to children and grandchildren of all California immigrants. These writers, though writing from a specific cultural context, must be seen as individuals. To quote Alfred Kazin from *On Native Grounds:*

> Though we are all bound up in society, we can never forget that literature is not practiced by "society" but by a succession of individuals and out of individual sensibility and knowledge and craft.

Chinese-Californian literature is composed of individual works by men and women who are Chinese-Americans but who are, more importantly, individuals working with individual memories of love and loss, triumph and pain. The argument between Frank Chin and Maxine Hong Kingston does not need to have a winner or loser. Literature is not about winning or losing but about the attempt to find our individual truth that is, yet, about more than ourselves.

CHAPTER 12

Fat City: A California Classic

Leonard Gardner

A major California and American novel, Leonard Gardner's *Fat City,* was published more than 40 years ago. As was noted by novelist Gerald Haslam, *"Fat City* gave many Americans their first look at the Central Valley...since *The Grapes of Wrath."* Gardner's novel, and the movie that followed, graced by Gardner's screenplay, fulfilled the promise of California's heartland writing; Gardner, in his very mastery of concrete detail and immersion in place, in his compassion for the down and heartbroken, became an artist of universal power. Like William Saroyan in his identification with the Armenian survivors of genocide living in Fresno, and like Steinbeck in his great sympathy for the dust-bowl migrants, Gardner writes about Northern California in such a way that we understand the pain of not just one place, but of the whole world.

Gardner's sense of setting is his great strength. He is both impressionistic and realistic. It is 1959. Stockton is a port city, a train terminus, a skid row nightmare. Okies, Mexicans, Blacks, Chinese, Filipinos walk the hard streets beneath brick hotels. Stockton, 84 road miles from San Francisco, could be 840 miles from the City in terms of mood and psychological fact. From the novel's opening paragraph, Gardner demonstrates knowledge and mastery of place.

> From his window he looked out on the stunted skyline of Stockton—a city of 80,000 surrounded by sloughs, rivers, and fertile fields of the San Joaquin River...

Gardner expertly contrasts the fertility of the valley with the impotence and loss in the streets.

Along the sidewalk under his window men passed between bars and liquor stores, cafes, secondhand stores and walk-up hotels...

Gardner's contrast emphasizes his major theme; that what could have been, or should have been, has been drowned in the misery of what is. *Fat City*'s central character, boxer Billy Tully, could have been champion of the world, but is, in fact, a 29-year-old skid row alcoholic. The great valley itself, once a place of fertility and promise, is now the setting where farm laborers struggle with the short-handled hoe. Stockton, a Gold Rush city at founding, is now *Fat City*, a place of shattered dreams.

In *The Grapes of Wrath*, Ma Joad, speaking for thousands of Okies, stated that, "...All we got is the family unbroken..." Now Tully, son of Dust Bowl refugees, is totally estranged from his father and family, poverty is both physical and emotional. Tully's father is described thus:

A small red-faced alcoholic cement finisher with brown teeth and an Oklahoma accent, the old man had got up from the bed, gone home and got drunk. On the back porch, after a shouted quarrel with his father, Tully had left...He had left them behind, Tully told himself, the only one still here in the city where they had last lived together.

Tully, nearly 30 and going down slow, is contrasted with Ernie Munger, a decade younger, a man who has some of the same dreams that Tully once owned. Munger's relationship with his girlfriend and future wife, Fay, gives further evidence of Gardner's use of setting to demonstrate the duality of both nature and human nature, of man caught between the promise of heaven and the reality of hell: "With Fay crushed against him, he drove between the hot fields to Lodi or Tracy or Modesto, where they turned around to come back...." Ernie wants to both leave Fay and to stay with her forever. She represents both hopeless entanglement and true passage into manhood: "Later, on her front porch, she looked so lovely to him, so graceful, that he could not turn and go home." Stockton, too, is both a fertile place of promise, and a desolate and sad Western city, a true trap, empty of hope.

Gardner's exploration of fieldwork moves beyond observation to witness. Here, Gardner forgets duality; for, like Steinbeck, Gardner writes to correct injustice. Once again, man has exploited fellow man.

> They arrived at a field where the day's harvesting had already begun, and embracing an armload of sack, Tully ran with the others for the nearest row...He scrabbled on under the arc of sun, cutting and tossing.

Unlike Steinbeck's Okies, who have a strong identity, Gardner's laborers are individual. They work in pairs, ignorant of their exploitation. "...Negro paired with Negro white and white, Mexican with Mexican, and Filipino beside Filipino..." Tully, unlike Steinbeck's Tom Joad and Preacher Casy, can see himself only in his individual pain. While using the (since outlawed) short-handled hoe, Tully thinks that "...he could not go on even another hour. He felt his existence had come to final halt...and he felt being white no longer made any difference..."

Tragedy, for Gardner, is defined as suffering without friendship. Suffering in isolation without love, Gardner shows, is truly hell on earth. Tully's clumsy attempt to make Ernie his friend is Tully's last chance to find humanity and community.

Gardner emphasizes Tully's tragedy by contrasting Tully with Lucero, a Mexican boxer, Tully's opponent during his comeback. Lucero has the community that Tully lacks.

> He had gained ten pounds since the photo was taken. Even so, he entered, it was evident the bartender recognized him. Lucero found the faces of his countrymen turning to look at him, and he felt at home, as at home as he ever felt anywhere...

Tully, unlike Lucero, has been stripped of roots. Within California writing, Saroyan's Fresno Armenians, Steinbeck's Oklahomans, Gary

Soto's Mexican-Americans, Maya Angelou's Blacks, all have a past and culture they can love and hate—that helps them survive. But neither of Gardner's heroes have the consolation of culture. Billy Tully ends up alone in skid row, where, beneath the clamor of drunken argument and angry sex, exists the terrible stillness of despair. Gardner knows this life, which exists still, downtown, just a short drive away from the homes of the old and new California suburbs.

Gardner's very real accomplishment is to restore a sense of dignity to the fallen men and women, who, too, once had real dreams, ambition, hope. Gardner knows that loss can be written about and understood. He has made *Fat City* a compassionate metaphor for all who have fought blindly and alone and have, in their aloneness, truly failed. And those of us outside skid row, Gardner knows, are not exempt.

More than 40 years following its publication, *Fat City* stands with a handful of post-World War II American classics. The novel would be a worthy addition to any course dealing with American or West Coast literature.

CHAPTER 13

Jack Kerouac and the California Dream

J ack Kerouac was not born in California. Nor would he live in California for any extended period of time. Yet Kerouac is an important California writer. Kerouac's two most important California prose works, "The Mexican Girl" (a section from *On the Road)* and the autobiographical *Big Sur* are definitive statements relating to the myth of California.

Kerouac's California becomes not a Beat heaven nor a hippie Eden but an American place, humanized by loss and tears. Unlike fellow Beats Allen Ginsburg, Lawrence Ferlinghetti, Michael McClure, Gary Snyder, and in opposition to Haight Street heroes Ken Kesey, Richard Brautigan, and Tim Leary, Kerouac did not believe that hip California had ushered in a change of human consciousness. Kerouac, an honest writer, knew better. His prose details experience with the other California, that place of struggle and broken dreams and loss that exists so poignantly beneath our romantic false image of ourselves.

Influenced by Saroyan and Steinbeck, a traveler in the romantic tradition of Jack London, Kerouac's response was to the beauty of landscape and the tenderness of people. He reacted to California first with the awe and wonder of a tourist in Eden, before understanding finally the nature of his experience in California, experience that would leave the writer resigned to the universality of human suffering.

"The Mexican Girl" is a crucial part of *On the Road.* Kerouac published the passage separately as a story in "New World Writing" (1955), and the prose serves as a self-portrait of Kerouac in 1947, at the age of 25.

Hitchhiking from Oakland through the San Joaquin Valley, young Kerouac (Sal Paradise in the novel) is intoxicated by place.

> All the magic names of the valley unrolled...Manteca,
> Madera, and the rest. Soon it got...the fields the color

of love and Spanish mysteries...it was the most beautiful of moments.

Next to Thomas Wolfe, William Saroyan was Kerouac's strongest literary influence, and in Fresno, Kerouac walks by himself and thinks of Saroyan. Significantly, it is in Fresno that Kerouac truly begins to perceive Saroyan's California, the melancholy beneath the exuberance and humor.

> I went for a quick coke in a little grocery store by the tracks and here came a melancholy Armenian youth along the red boxcars, and just at that moment a locomotive howled and I said to myself, "Yes, Yes, Saroyan's town."

Fresno becomes then, for Kerouac, both a reminder of and warning against Spanish mysteries.

In Bakersfield, Kerouac meets the girl who will change his life: "I was waiting for the L.A. bus when all of a sudden I saw the cutest little Mexican girl in slacks come cutting across my sight." Hesitant, Kerouac asks the girl if he can sit with her. Soon he is in heaven: "Without coming to any particular agreement we began holding hands! I ached all over for her! I leaned my head in her beautiful hair." The Greyhound rolls into Los Angeles. Northern California has been left behind. Kerouac paints a word picture of the strangeness of L.A. He has left Northern California for another country. "...I looked greedily out the window; stucco houses and palms and drive-ins, the whole mad thing, the ragged promised land, the fantastic end of America..."

> L.A., though, is a false promise. We got off the bus at Main Street, which was no different from where you get off the bus in Kansas City or Chicago or Boston—red brick, dirty, characters drifting by, trolleys grating in the hopeless dawn, the whorey smells of a big city.

Instead of Spanish mysteries, Kerouac has started a love affair with a young mother, a woman who has left her young son with relatives in the San Joaquin Valley. Kerouac can keep his illusion of excitement only in Los Angeles, which he recognizes as being unreal. Central Avenue is described thus: "What a wild place it is, with chicken shacks barely big enough to house a jukebox and the jukebox blowing nothing but blues, bop, and jump...."

Back in the San Joaquin Valley, back in Northern California, reality has taken hold. Looking east to the Sierra, picking cotton, Kerouac is unable to be of any help to his girl, Terry, or her son. Kerouac's love has become a sad joke. So have his promises to his "girl."

An honest recorder, the young man from Lowell, Massachusetts, has become a California writer. He now understands the pain he only sensed while reading London and Saroyan and Steinbeck. Northern California, still a delight to his senses, will not be an escape. Spanish mysteries exist side by side with deserted young mothers and melancholy, disappointed young men.

Kerouac's Big Sur

> I was alone with this mad beatnik kid singing me songs and all I wanta do is sleep—But I've got to make the best of it and not disappoint his believing heart.

> Because after all the poor kid actually believes that there's something noble and idealistic and kind about all this beat stuff, and I'm supposed to be the King of the Beatniks according to the newspapers, so but at the same time...my reason for coming to Big Sur for the summer being precisely to get away from that sort of thing....

Published in 1962, Kerouac's confessional novel *Big Sur* illuminates the 1960s. Kerouac's testimony is particularly relevant to those of us who persist in glorifying the North Beach scene of the late 1950s and the counterculture that erupted in 1967 in the Haight-Ashbury district of San Francisco.

Big Sur opens in August of 1960. "The Beat Generation" has taken hold everywhere since Kerouac's publication of *On the Road* in 1957 but nowhere is the myth of the Beat life more seductive than North Beach in San Francisco. Young readers—from Arizona to Kansas to Maine—have come to San Francisco to live the life they had read about in *On the Road*.

Yet Kerouac, "King of the Beats," is no longer 25 years old. His friend Neal Cassady (Dean Moriarty of *On the Road,* Cody in *Big Sur*) has served two years in San Quentin for possession of marijuana. Literary success seems to have accelerated Kerouac's alcoholism and Kerouac himself returns to California—not as a pied piper of youth, but as a desperate man who seeks a last chance to recover health and balance.

Here, again, Kerouac confronts the truth of the California dream. In 1947 he was a road kid and seeker; in the later 1950s (the time of *Dharma Bums* and *Desolation Angels*) he came to California as a poet and a representative of a literary movement, but at age 38 he returns seeking a last chance at life. Lawrence Ferlinghetti has offered Kerouac the use of his cabin at Bixby Canyon. Kerouac—realizing the severity of his situation—knows that if he can begin to recover at Bixby Canyon, then he may live, not die, in middle age. Kerouac's California dream is a world away from the dreams of his contemporaries: "...No more dissipation, it's time for me to quietly watch the world and even enjoy it...no booze, no drugs, no bouts with beatniks and junkies..." Wild Northern California becomes, for Kerouac, truly a place of last hope.

In *Big Sur* Kerouac is forced to understand that his healing will not come from his position as Beat hero, San Francisco poet, or North Beach celebrity. He is forced to see that California will not by itself grant inner peace. He must confront Northern California as it is in 1960—with its spreading suburbs, pretentious hipsters, and with its racial tensions.

His friend, Neal Cassady, has, too, become less romantic. California society has changed since *On the Road* and Cassady's knowledge is prison knowledge. Driving the Bayshore Freeway, Kerouac and Cassady pick up a hitchhiker, an old man who tells the pair that "…he'd just been beaten by a gang of young Negroes for no reason in a public toilet and Cody gasps to me…I've met those Negroes that beat up old men, they're called strongarms in San Quentin…" This sad knowledge is accepted by the man who rhapsodied in *On the Road* about "wishing I could exchange worlds with the happy, true hearted ecstatic Negroes in America…"

Kerouac cannot make it alone at Big Sur. After a week, he returns to San Francisco with Neal Cassady and in the city becomes involved with a woman as unstable as himself. Sex brings confusion and pain. Young Kerouac, in *On the Road,* had been able to feel sympathy and love for his Mexican girl, Terry, as shown in this famous passage from that novel:

> In reverent and sweet little silence she took all her clothes off and slipped her tiny body into the sheets with me. It was brown as grapes. I saw her poor belly where there was a Cesarean scar; her hips were so narrow she couldn't bear a child without being gashed open…She was only four foot ten. I made love to her in the sweetness of the weary morning. Then, two tired angels having found the closest and most delicious thing in life together, we fell asleep and slept till late afternoon…

In 1960 in San Francisco, however, Kerouac finds not love but pretension, masquerade, and tragedy. Kerouac's new girlfriend, Billie, is a person Kerouac cannot trust, and her jargon reveals to Kerouac not tenderness but fake, hipster gamesmanship. Billie and her friends are "New Age" people before the term came into being. Kerouac's distrust is made explicit in the following passage:

> Billie and her gang, in fact, with all that fancy rigmarole about spiritual matters I wonder…I've noticed it before in San Francisco, a kind of ephemeral hysteria…leading always to suicide and maim…

With Billie, Kerouac weakly drinks and watches himself fall apart. During the worst night of his life, with others at Bixby Canyon, Kerouac's D.T.'s are finally quelled through a vision of the cross, which calms the Catholic Kerouac and allows him to accept his fate. Kerouac travels back to New York City, not saved but also not condemned. He would not travel to California again and never would he laud what came to be known as the counterculture.

Kerouac was not surprised at the failure of hippie community. For Kerouac viewed critically both conventional society, a place where he could not fit, and the hip life, which he realized was no salve for anyone's individual pain.

Before the decade was out, thousands traveled to California to learn a truth Kerouac had already detailed. Kerouac came to the end of his road in California. Here, listening to the Pacific, hitchhiking the Great Valley, walking San Francisco, Kerouac confronted the truth of his own life. In his tears, with his confession, Kerouac speaks to and for many more than himself.

Kerouac's California was not the place of counterculture myth. Like every major figure of California writing, like Jack London, like William Saroyan, like John Steinbeck, Kerouac found in California a mirror of the human condition; California offered the hope of youth, not utopian solution.

Kerouac's California lives in his writing as a place where young women and young men walk beneath the stars, not free of their pain or mortality, not relieved by drink or drug or easy talk.

CHAPTER 14

Of Culture and Anarchy

Joan Didion Sees Dark Side of the Summer of Love

"…The love of our neighbor, the impulse toward action, help, and beneficence, the desire for removing error, clearing human confusion, and diminishing human misery, the noble aspiration to leave the world better and happier than we found it—motives, eminently such as called social, come in as part of the grounds of culture, and the main and pre-eminent part…"

—*Matthew Arnold*, Culture and Anarchy, *1868*

"…Here are some particulars. At midnight, last night, on the road in from Las Vegas to Death Valley Junction, a car hit a shoulder and turned over. The driver, very young and apparently drunk, was killed instantly. His girl was found alive but bleeding internally, deep in shock. I talked this afternoon to the nurse who had driven the girl to the nearest doctor, 185 miles across the floor of the valley and three ranges of lethal mountain road. The nurse explained that her husband, a talc miner, had stayed on the highway with the boy's body until the coroner could get over the mountains from Bishop, at dawn today. 'You just can't leave a body on the highway,' she said. 'It's immoral.'

"It was one instance in which I did not distrust the word…"

—*Joan Didion*, On Morality, *1965*

Reading Matthew Arnold's nineteenth-century essay, *Culture and Anarchy*, made me think of the American writer whose moral concerns echo Matthew Arnold—Joan Didion. A century after Arnold published *Culture and Anarchy*—dealing with the crisis in values of English industrial society—Didion, in a trio of essays in her collection, *Slouching Toward Bethlehem*, wrote about similar issues confronting our explosive, expanding modern California, where the demand for social order confronted the desire for absolute personal freedom. The issues Didion explored are all with us still. For we have not resolved the debate between those who believe culture means control and those who argue that freedom must have no limits. Didion and Arnold have no exact answers but they write out of the desire to see our lives in a moral context. And by morality they do not mean the word in an abstract way; they are not talking about beautiful words but about beautiful deeds. Didion, like Arnold, felt that we must, as individuals, be responsible to each other as members of the human family, that we must judge one another as individuals, and crucially, that we must reject the easy slogans of both liberal and conservative.

We must, thought Arnold, create a culture composed of people who have "...the moral and social passion for doing good." Doing good, for Arnold, led to actions that visibly demonstrate caring. Didion's insight was to understand, 100 years after Arnold, that doing good is demonstrated by acts not words. As she wrote prophetically in 1965, "...all the ad-hoc committees, all the picket lines, all the brave signatures to the *New York Times*...do not confer virtue...."

Arnold believed, and here he speaks to us directly, that a culture could not be created by those who have a need to "indoctrinate the masses with the set of ideas and judgment constituting the creed of their own profession or party...."

What does this mean for us today?

As teachers, and especially as teachers of English, we work at a time when all around us—the politically correct of the left and the patriotically correct of the right—have done their best to indoctrinate, to dictate, and to deny basic freedom of inquiry. The hard left and hard right wish to dictate their own conception of culture and to brand as anarchic or subversive what they do not agree with. From right-wingers who refuse to teach Marx or Darwin or Alice Walker, to left-wingers who deny a place in the curriculum to *Huckleberry Finn*, we have been teaching in a time in which culture has been defined in narrow, parochial terms and which anarchy has been the word to describe dissenting ideas.

Our answer, in simplest terms, is to oppose indoctrination with an introduction to critical thinking. We can choose books for our students that open more questions than give exact answers—and we can give writing assignments, on issues like Affirmative Action—that encourage opponents to understand that on some issues right opposes right, that debate does not mean demonization. We can remember that we teach a form that explodes the myth of easy answer.

Thus, Huckleberry Finn, discovering that his best and only real friend, a Black slave, is more important to him than following the rules of Southern slave society. Thus, Malcolm X, discovering at Mecca that whites can be his brothers and that the "brother" he idolized, Elijah Muhammad, was an enemy, not a friend. Thus, J.D. Salinger's Holden Caulfield, betrayed by his former teacher, a man he once trusted, and helped by the nuns of a religion he has mistrusted. Literature defies stereotypes, makes abstract ideas specific, allows us to seek honestly our personal place in the world.

Literature takes away from the idea that phrases like "the Christian majority," "right to life," "people of color," or "pro-choice," confer sainthood. Literature—reading and writing—take us away from easy dismissal of others.

Which leads me to Joan Didion and the importance of what she wrote one generation ago. For Didion fulfilled, in *Slouching Toward Bethlehem*, the writer's obligations not to accept abstractions but to look for the concrete reality. In "Dreamers of the Lost Dream," Didion wrote about a fundamentalist Christian community in Southern California, a middle-class community defined finally by cheating, blackmail, and murder. She described a world where religion is the thinnest of veneers. That world seemed a light year from the hippies of the Haight-Ashbury but Didion, in the spring of 1967, travels to the Haight, where she finds, as she did in "Dreamers of the Lost Dream," not love but talk of love. She finds abandonment and people using each other. She quotes Chester Anderson, an eyewitness, to make her point, to press her argument, and she did so when the media were romanticizing the hippies. From *Slouching Toward Bethlehem*:

> Pretty little sixteen-year-old middle-class chick comes to the Haight to see what it's all about and gets picked up by a seventeen-year-old street dealer who spends all day shooting her full of speed again and again and then raffles her off... for the biggest Haight Street gang bang since the night before last... The politics of ethics as ecstasy. Rape is as common as bullshit on Haight Street. Kids are starving on the Street. Minds and bodies are being maimed as we watch, a scale model of Vietnam...

What unites the conservative Christians and the hippies, Didion finds, is the use of words as justification. "It was, moreover, in the name of 'love'; everyone involved placed a magic faith in the efficacy of the very word."

Didion's essay, "On Morality," shows not empty words of love but actions that demonstrate concern and care. A nurse and her husband, in the 118-degree heat of the California desert, stay with the body of a man they do not know, care for his hurt woman companion. "We stay with the body," writes Didion, "or we have bad dreams."

Literature, great writing, is not liberal or conservative, religious or secular; it is an art that, at best, connects us with the pain of other humans and leads us toward doing the right thing. We, as teachers of literature, can lead students toward a culture based upon respecting others and seeing ourselves in others. We can reject indoctrination and stereotype.

As for now, our culture is shallow and the anarchy we see—what is violence but anarchy?—is a measure of our failure.

A humane culture identifies itself, as Arnold stated, by "love of our neighbor, the impulse to help." We cannot reach this goal by making literature servant of party, gender, religion, or race.

CHAPTER 15

From Oakland to Oaktown

Hugh Pearson and Jess Mowry

"During the Sixties, this myth of the redeemed criminal had a tremendous influence on our young people, when criminals guilty of every crime, from con games to rape, to murder exploited it by declaring themselves political activists and Black leaders. As a result, many sincere dedicated leaders of an older generation were swept aside. I'm speaking now of courageous individuals who made sacrifices in order to master the disciplines of leadership and who created a continuity between themselves and earlier leaders of our struggle. The kids treated such people as if they were Uncle Toms, and I found it outrageous. Because not only did it distort the historical difference between one period of struggle and another, it made heroes out of thugs and self-servers out of dedicated leaders…"

—*Ralph Ellison in conversation with Ishmael Reed, Steven Cannon, and Quincy Troupe in "Y Bird," reprinted in* The Pushcart Prize, III

After Huey Newton was shot dead in West Oakland, in August of 1989, he was eulogized as a race leader, as a king. The much-admired Rev. Cecil Williams of San Francisco's Glide Memorial Church orated at Newton's funeral.

Left out of the oration were some salient facts; never mind that Newton was killed as part of a cocaine turf war. Never mind that Newton had—without reason, among other crimes—pistol-whipped a Black tailor (whose crime was to call Newton "baby"). Never mind that Newton had murdered an African-American prostitute, organized a shakedown of small businessmen of his own community, used and abused a number of women.

He was still, in the Bay Area and elsewhere, a hero to the remnant of the New Left and the remains of Black Power. It was left to a working-class Black woman (first quoted by Ken Kelly in the *East Bay Express* and later noted by Hugh Pearson in his excellent *The Shadow of the Panther*) to place Newton in perspective.

"If Huey was Moses," the woman said, "give me old Pharaoh Ramses anytime."

And yet now, not that many years after Newton's death, a one-man-play extolling Huey has been performed in Oakland to the positive reviews of the same *East Bay Express* while the politically correct left is reflected by the following response to Newton's life and death in the same paper. Neither Ken Kelly's journalism or Hugh Pearson's book will convince those who believe, to quote the *Express* letter:

> We remember the Huey Newton who stood up strong
> and black, who faced down the pigs and scared the shit
> out of the racists whose worst nightmares seemed to
> come true...

Now Newton exists in the romantic memory haze of another time. Of course, it is obscene to compare Newton with Dr. King or Malcolm X. Yet who would have predicted that Louis Farrakhan would be seen as a legitimate race leader, or that Rosa Parks, Maya Angelou, or Jesse Jackson would share a stage with him?

Hugh Pearson: *The Shadow of the Panther*

In the face of this revisionist time, Hugh Pearson's book, *The Shadow of the Panther*, is more than a corrective. It must not have been an easy book to write. For a Black writer, a man who idolized Newton as a boy, a writer aware of the continued existence of white racism, it must not have been pleasant to document the actions of a murderer, not a savior. But if Pearson reveals that Newton is no hero, he finds in the African-

American community of Oakland, and elsewhere, Ellison's truly coura-geous individuals.

Pearson's book is a history of Negro Oakland and the long strug-gle for acceptance and equality that, eventually, produced a man and a movement that promised so much and delivered so little. For, as Pearson makes clear, it was ultimately not the police or the F.B.I. that destroyed Newton and the Black Panther Party. It was the Panthers themselves and thus a suffering community was betrayed once again. Pearson takes the reader on an exploration of Black Oakland, the West Oakland ghetto in particular, and he makes telling points about historic Negro life, about the men and women who migrated to Oakland from the segregated South, most especially Texas, Louisiana, and Arkansas. He writes about leaders like C. L. Dellums, of the Sleeping Car Porters Union, a right-hand assistant to A. Philip Randolph and the uncle of for-mer Berkeley congressman and Oakland mayor, Ron Dellums. Pearson details the effect of those who fought for jobs and equality in Oakland before and during Newton's time. Specifically, by the early 1960s, the fight centered around job opportunity, focusing upon the giant Lucky chain, as well as direct action protests against San Francisco's Sheraton Palace Hotel. Other actions moved toward ending housing discrimi-nation. These attempts were coordinated with CORE as well as U.C. Berkeley's activist organizations, and the protesters were both Black and white. Many of the protests were successful in breaking down the lines of discrimination.

Everything changed during the 1960s and early on, in *The Shadow of the Panther*, Pearson comes to a crucial insight about the inability of many sympathetic whites to differentiate between Black political prison-ers and Black criminals.

> ...included among the ranks of such men (Black pris-oners) were those who would be criminals even without the existence of Jim Crow. Every community had such criminals and the middle- and working-class Negroes wanted no connection with them—the ones who cut each other up inside and outside the pool halls and bar-

rooms or stole from and killed other people, primarily other Negroes.

Pearson writes of the later 1960s, explaining the appeal of the Panthers to the student radicals of the SDS as well as the radical chic in Hollywood and New York.

Pearson writes:

> As the movement gained ground, the line separating such criminals from Negroes who were unjustly imprisoned would become blurred beyond recognition by the increasingly radicalized Negro college students spending time in jail for their Civil Rights activity. And later their young northern white allies would further help blur the line...

Pearson thus places Huey Newton and the Black Panthers in the context of a national racial movement for equality that disintegrated into a movement of violence. For Panthers to grab the national spotlight, Martin Luther King Jr. and his young, brave followers, like John Lewis and Robert Moses, would have to be eclipsed. That battle between men like Lewis and Stokely Carmichael would have tragic consequences as the Black Power movement moved north. Pearson does not slight the conditions that led to Black Power, the nightmare conditions of the deep South or the de-facto segregation of the North. Pearson documents Black mistreatment in Oakland, comparing such treatment to the way "Okies" had similarly been prejudiced against in California's great Central Valley.

> Oakland whites had not expected Negroes to stay after the war, much less continue to arrive from the South in large numbers. They panicked in much the same way that earlier white settlers panicked when white 'Okies' poured into California during the Great Depression...

Oakland was a city with a large Black ghetto in West Oakland, a place of racial segregation and a place where a nearly all-white police force had amassed a record of police brutality. Pearson writes about conditions that helped, by 1965 and 1967, allow white and Black revolutionaries to seize the day over the established civil rights community. Oakland, initially, was just one of the focal points in the battle over Black leadership.

Pearson shows how Stokely Carmichael's and H. Rap Brown's challenge to Martin Luther King Jr. helped the Black Panthers amass power in Oakland. And men like Carmichael, Brown, and Newton would seize the day over men and women who had struggled a lifetime for racial equality. The older leaders would see young Blacks and whites sabotage a movement, as the Black and white radicals denigrated their elders as Uncle Toms.

Pearson writes about a media fascinated by gun-toting Black Panthers and the civil rights coalition led by Dr. King would play a terrible price.

And in the Bay Area, whites and Blacks who had together challenged and ended segregation would be denigrated. Ending segregation was not what Black Power or the Black Panthers were about.

Pearson writes about writer-activist-comedian Dick Gregory, who was impressed with the pre-Panther Bay Area coalition of white and Black. Pearson includes the following Gregory quote:

> For eighteen months I was able to see no hope at all...I think now the answer to the Negro problem lies here—in the San Francisco formula. Seventy-four percent of the civil rights demonstrators are white. There can't be any race riots here or bloodshed because there are so many whites working for us...

But the escalation of the war in Vietnam and the radicalization of young whites would have disastrous consequences for Oakland and America. And Huey Newton, an intelligent, handsome sociopath, conman and murderer, would move from strength to strength, lionized by the children of the white upper middle and middle classes, lionized by the radical elites.

Newton would be involved in hard drugs, order murder, and live the high life with his Hollywood friends. Meanwhile he would consolidate his power by viciously abusing even his former friends; witness his treatment of Black Panther co-founder Bobby Seale, with whom Newton was involved in a power struggle for control of the Black Panther Party. Newton would stop at nothing in order to consolidate his power and to affirm his position as undisputed leader. Here, again, in *The Shadow of the Panther*, Pearson writes:

> ... Newton dramatically beat Seale with a bullwhip and sodomized him so viciously that his anus had to be surgically repaired by a physician who was a party sympathizer. Seale left town, went into hiding, and wasn't heard from at least a year, when he turned up in Philadelphia, never to have anything again to do with the party...

Pearson's narrative is tragic. For while Newton amassed personal power (and the Seale incident is typical of Newton's violent ways of getting control), his people suffered and legitimate leaders were brushed aside. Pearson has written a brutally painful and truthful book about Oakland, California, and about a time whose consequences we pay for still.

Jess Mowry: *Way Past Cool*

Jess Mowry was born in 1960 in Mississippi and raised in Oakland. He is a novelist and short story writer of power. His short story, "Animal Rights," is a masterpiece. In some ways, Mowry described an Oakland not too different from Richard Wright's or Nelson Algren's Chicago. But Mowry's indictment of individuals—not society but individuals, in this case liberal whites and Blacks—is different from Wright's and Algren's condemnation of society. For within society, Wright and Algren found individuals worthy of respect and hope.

Mowry describes a world of desertion. The young Blacks in *Way Past Cool* have been deserted by family, society, schools, and all adults.

Mowry's novel features characters who are intelligent, verbal, street smart, and who believe with the author that "white" society does not care if they live or die. Mowry's characters' speeches seem to be the polemics of the author and put-down of teachers (of all races and ethnicities) is complete:

> "Too fuckin funny, man! Ain't one of them stupid teachers gotta live around here. Not know from nothing what is. Shit, this goddamn English story too...how I gonna spend my motherfuckin summer vacation! Been bustin my goddamn ass over it all cocksuckin week, and now old Crabzilla gonna kill me for sure.... We gonna be late an get tardies up the wazoo!"

This speech is accurate and I, as a teacher, have heard variations of it from middle-class children too—of all colors—but unlike the author, I do not believe the hostility of youth to have found an accurate target.

Mowry's novel reflects the way the 1980s and 1990s have grown out of the worst part of the 1960s and 1970s. Mowry does not believe that individuals outside of the circle of neighborhood or race or class care about or want to help ease the suffering of others. But contrary to his belief, there are caring teachers, white and brown and Asian and African-American, in East and West Oakland, and I have met some of them. Mowry's indictment is too total, at its worst, a direct line from Newton and Cleaver and the white radicals of the SDS with their most extreme rhetorical simplifications and lies.

Mowry may be too young to remember Mississippi Summer, but he is not too young to know about the many whites who risked their lives for the cause of equality. And what about those whites in Oakland and the Bay Area who marched and picketed and were arrested for the cause of ending segregation? And what of the Blacks in Oakland who moved from the South, who protested peacefully, who taught, and nursed, and coached and worked and did their best to raise their families in dignity?

Mowry's novel has great power and great limitations. But his portraits of the bravest as well as the most criminal of Oakland youth should not be ignored. His heroes find love as well as violent death. At his best Mowry has given faceless children a place of dignity, and in his short story, "Animal Rights" (from *Where Coyotes Howl and the Wind Blows Free*, University of Nevada Press), his indictment of cruelty is beyond race. It is a universal indictment of both a society that cares more about whales than children, and parents, in this case an inner-city father, who cares more about drugs and drug money than his own son. For the problems of California and its many Oaktowns, Mowry is not bound to offer a solution.

Conclusion

In 1979, the summer I prepared to quit the Main Oakland Post Office, located in the slums of West Oakland, not far from where Newton would eventually be killed, I used to see him. I was living in North Oakland, and Newton sometimes ordered lunch at the Smokehouse on Telegraph Avenue, the same place I would walk to for lunch before my shift—Tour 3 began.

Everyone gave Newton a wide berth. He arrived with his bodyguard, a huge man with a shaven head. Newton, himself, was leather-jacketed, handsome, charismatic, always in motion, very frightening. He was a man who quite obviously could easily kill; and in that sense, he was a street gangster and a true revolutionary of the 20th century, like Castro or Mao or Che.

In 1980, during the fall, I worked for CETA as a writing tutor at Berkeley High School. We worked, before the Reagan Administration ended funding, teaching basic writing skills to mainly Black kids from Berkeley's flatlands. We also taught Latinos, Vietnamese, whites. We were paid less than six dollars an hour for a full day's work. We were women and men in our late 20s and early 30s, of all races, who wanted to be teachers. We had the "naïve" belief that teaching reading and writing and literature could do some good in the world. And a high school teacher I remain.

Meanwhile, famous veterans of the New Left and Black Power returned to universities, gained tenure, wrote books. White and Black radicals, they celebrate themselves. They do so still. They say they care about the "people." But the people, as Mowry shows—and their children in West and East Oakland and the other inner cities of the nation—are more demoralized, more hopeless, and more betrayed than ever. They wait and they have waited. Let us celebrate the brave among their elders who have tried, as Hugh Pearson shows, to improve these children's lives. Let us remember the Blacks and whites who together, a generation ago, broke down the walls of segregation.

From Newton and the Panthers, from the drive-by gangsters of our time, from academic radicals, they have received no real help at all.

CHAPTER 16

Native California Revisited

Scott Momaday, Thomas Sanchez,
Greg Sarris, Malcolm Margolin

"I mean our history, Alice. Look at what the Spanish did, then the Mexicans, then the Americans. All of them, they took our land, locked us up. Then look at what we go and do to one another…"

—*Greg Sarris, "The Water Place," Grand Avenue*

"Most people deceive themselves with a pair of faiths; they believe in eternal memory (of people, things, deeds, nations) and in redeemability (of deeds, mistakes, sins, wrongs). Both are false faiths. Everything will be forgotten and nothing will be redeemed…"

—*Milan Kundera*

Since the 1960s, a number of novels, short stories, poems, biographical sketches, and essays have been written by Native Americans and others to remember Indian history and to disprove that view of life stated so forcefully by Kundera.

These writers of Native American and Native California life believe, to again quote Gregory Sarris, "Talk. It's important to talk. Us Indians here are all family. That's the trouble, no one talks. Stories, the true stories, that's what we need to hear…"

Scott Momaday in *House Made of Dawn*, Thomas Sanchez in *Rabbit Boss*, Greg Sarris in *Grand Avenue*, Bev Ortiz in *News from Native California*, and Suzanne Abel-Vidor, Dot Brovarney, Susan Billy, Malcolm Margolin, and others in *Remember Your Relations* have written stories and memoirs so that not everything will be forgotten. They have written in the hope, too, that some wrongs might be redeemed.

These works, all set in California, seek to make of Native California life more than a commemoration. The descendants of the first Americans living in California face the same essential conflicts of all of us who have an ancestral heritage, language, and religion. How can we honor our past without being dominated by it? How do we resolve our multiple loyalties and identities? How can Native Californians reconcile tribal religion with Christianity? Contemporary California with the history of the Indian peoples of California?

Scott Momaday: *House Made of Dawn*

Scott Momaday is not a Californian. He is a Kiowa Indian. One of the strongest passages in *House Made of Dawn* is an autobiographical passage about a man's journey from California to bury his Kiowa grandmother in Oklahoma.

House Made of Dawn, published in 1968, takes place between 1945 and 1952 in Southern California, in "Wakatola, Canton of San Diego," and in Los Angeles. The novel's central character is named Abel. He is a war hero, a murderer, a lover, an alcoholic—who ultimately finds sanity through a return to Native American tradition.

The novel is especially impressive in its originality of characters. None of the characters, white or Indian, are mere stereotypes. The non-Indian characters are especially interesting. For example, Father Olguin, the village priest, is a man sympathetic to Indians. After Abel kills a white man during a peyote ceremony who interrupts Abel and his friends, and who Abel believes to be the incarnation of evil, the priest pleads for Abel in court. He is, in Norman Maclean's eloquent words, able to express "complete love without complete understanding."

Angela, the white doctor's wife who becomes Abel's lover, will, though she has returned to her husband, visit Abel when he is hospitalized in Los Angeles seven years after their affair has ended. She gives to Abel, despite her limitations, as much as she can give. What she cannot give, finally, is herself. What she can do is help lead Abel back toward his own people. Here, in the hospital, she speaks to Abel of the child who may be Abel's son.

> "Peter [her son] always asked her about the Indians, she said, and she used to tell him a story about a young Indian brave. He was born of a bear and a maiden, she said, and he has many adventures and he became a great leader and saved his people. It was the story Peter liked best and she always thought of him, Abel, when she told it..."

Milly, the daughter of the Dust Bowl, who lives with Abel in Los Angeles, is able to express love—albeit a love Abel cannot fully accept. She is not false, however, and her feelings for Abel, recently released from prison, are painfully real.

The novel is told through multiple narrators—as in Faulkner's *Sound and the Fury*—and like Faulkner, Momaday believes in the possibility of atonement and reconciliation.

Momaday tells the reader that, in their hearts, the Indians have not forgotten their ancestral ways.

> They do not hanker after progress and have never changed their essential way of life. Their invaders were a long time in conquering them; and now after four centuries of Christianity, they still pray in Tanoan to old deities of the earth and sky and make their living from the things that are and always have been within their reach. They had assumed the names and gestures of their enemies but have held on to their own secret souls...

Abel's journey, which begins when he returns from World War II, is one toward recovering ancestral memory. As the novel opens, he had forgotten the old ways. His mother and father are dead and he cannot communicate with his grandfather. He has become mute when contemplating the Indian traditions.

> Abel walked into the canyon. His return to the town
> had been a failure, for all his looking forward. He had
> tried in the days that followed to speak to his grandfa-
> ther, but he could not say the things he wanted; he had
> tried to pray, to sing, to enter the into the old rhythm of
> the tongue, but he was no longer attuned to it....

At the novel's conclusion, Abel's grandfather's death brings Abel back to Walatowa from Los Angeles and brings him back home to himself. He "reached inside and placed his hands in the...crust and rubbed his arms and chest with ashes..."

He runs, remembering the ways and language—not of Roman Catholicism—but of his people's religion. "He had only the way of a song." And he realizes that the "house made of dawn" is the earth created by the Great Spirit, of which his grandfather is now a part. Writes Momaday:

> And he went running on the rise of the song. House
> made of pollen, house made of dawn. Qtsedalba.

Abel had become part of his grandfather's spirit.

Thomas Sanchez: *Rabbit Boss*

Rabbit Boss by Thomas Sanchez was published in 1971 and is a novel written in anger. Sanchez paints a picture of white racism and evil. The novel opens with a young Washo Indian observing the cannibalism of the Donner party, and many of the novels strongest passages show the continuance of white cruelty. An anthologized section (*California Heartland*—"Everywhere to Run, Nowhere to Hide," makes explicit Sanchez's belief that the treatment of Native Californians, of the Washo, was a crucifixion. "I am alone with you Christ...I am too cold to die. My ears bleed...Answer my soul, uncover the sign..."

In "Everywhere to Run," a Washo, hitchhiking from the High Sierra to San Francisco in 1924, is aware of his people's degradation. He is picked up by a man who unleashes a stream of racist comments about Indians, Mexicans, and "niggers," and he is left out at the Oakland terminal, "across the bay from the white buildings of San Francisco." But the young Indian can take no pleasure in the city. The earth itself has been crucified. The Indian narrates: "I made my way off the docks and felt the hard ground beneath my feet. They had covered the Earth with stone."

Sanchez's argument, like that of Momaday, centers around the knowledge that a lack of expression can, at times, mask an angry eloquence. They know that the native people are aware of what has been stolen from them and how they have been degraded. Momaday and Sanchez speak for those who have been rendered without a voice.

Greg Sarris: *Grand Avenue*

Sanchez's fusion of Native California religion and Christian imagery will be taken up in a less bitter way in Greg Sarris' *Grand Avenue*. Sarris knows what, in his case, the Pomo Indians have suffered historically. He is also interested in looking at what "what we go and do to one another." His picture of Grand Avenue in Santa Rosa during the 1960s renders a community defined by anger as well as caring, jealousy as well as compassion, waste as well as purpose. Sarris's characters achieve an earned sympathy from the reader. For the Pomos of his stories are far from idealized. They hurt one another, they sin but they practice atonement. The book is a novel of connected short stories—not unlike Sherwood Anderson's *Winesburg, Ohio,* or in California literature, Saroyan's *My Name is Aram* and Mori's *Yokohama, California.*

I found the whole collection compelling and especially liked two of the stories, "The Progress of this Disease," and "Secret Letters." In the first, a mother of six tries to comfort her daughter who is dying of cancer. Told in the first person, the story is bound with ideas of compassion and forgiveness. Suffering has brought the mother to a point of sympathy for fellow humans.

When Jeanne, the sick daughter, imitates her grandmother, saying "white people" with scorn, the narrator-mother replies, "Remember your Bible," I say. "All people are equal. Some just behave better."

Sarris, who is himself of mixed racial origins, finds in this story and others the theme of coping with human pain. We need strength in order to comfort, Sarris tells us, whether from the Bible or Pomo medicine— we need to care about one another. The story's end brings no miracle cure. At the story's conclusion, the mother, stopped at a red light, sees her and her daughter's reflection in the storefront window and states the universal truth, the truth that transcends race, the truth of a mother caring for and loving her suffering child. She sees "a mother and a daughter...a daughter slumped down, sick maybe or just sleeping...I continue home."

"Secret Letter" also packs a universal message. In "Secret Letter," a man, desperate to make contact with his illegitimate son, risks his own marriage to do right by his tangled bloodline. Again, a parent gives all of himself to atone, to do what is right. The specific Grand Avenue setting, Indians living in old army barracks in tenement-style poverty, makes real the places that enfold the human conflicts and resolutions.

"Secret Letter," as the other stories of *Grand Avenue,* is about people struggling to overcome their human limitations. The characters try to set wrongs right and become brave in their struggle to escape a tragic fate. Their struggle and essential bravery distinguishes this book from works that are only about victimhood.

Malcolm Margolin: *Remember Your Relations* and *News from Native California*

Malcolm Margolin is the publisher of both *News from Native California* and *Remember Your Relations* (Heyday Books). These publications make Native California life current and argue that the life of Native California is not a relic but totally contemporary. These true-life stories reveal Native Californians of rare character and artistry.

Remember Your Relations is co-published as a Catalogue by the Oakland Museum of California. Besides Margolin, who furnishes an introduction, the book is by three excellent writers, Suzanne Abel-Vidor, Dot "Brovarney" and Susan Billy. The book is subtitled *The Elsie Allen Baskets, Family and Friends* and reveals some of the most beautiful basketry the world has known, from the Pomo Indians. The books, too, introduce us to some extraordinary women, including Elsie Allen herself. Here we find contemporary Indians who have resolved some of the conflicts Momaday, Sanchez, and Sarris have written about. Elsie Allen, herself, for example, was both Roman Catholic and a practitioner of Pomo religion. She found, as did Sarris' character in "Disease," the universal aspects that unite humanity, when she decided to defy Pomo tradition in order to bring the secrets of Pomo basketry to the world. In this, she followed her mother who "became unhappy with this tradition that dictated the continual loss of material heritage. Recognizing the demands of a young family and her daughter's (Elsie's) disaffection with weaving would pass over the years, she told Elsie that her baskets should not be destroyed when she died…"

Mrs. Allen herself (from her autobiography) extended her mother's wishes and reached out to non-Native Californians.

> My daughter (Genevieve) visited me and wanted me to go with her to a Chinese restaurant where I expected to see none but Chinese eating. I was amazed to see other races eating there and saw also how proud they were of their own heritage. Since I felt that the Pomos were one of the greatest basket weavers in the world, I resolved in my heart that this wonderful art should not be lost and that I would learn it and teach others.

Thus, Elsie Camache Allen, the year before her mother's death and nearly 40 years after her grandmother's death, returned to basketmaking nearly full-time. The catalogue tells us that for the next 30 years she exhibited her work and "consulted for museums… taught basketweaving to Indian and non-Indian students."

Suzanne Abel-Vidor, Dot Brovarney, and Susan Billy are to be commended. Their writing profiles individual weavers such as Annie Ramon Burke, Mary Arnold, Mowsha Wilbell Edwards, and many others. These biographical sketches are living history, and one meets a succession of proud, dignified Pomo women, who, through basketry, have passed on the culture from generation to generation. The photographs within the catalogue give a sense of the intricacy and beauty of the baskets, as well as the depth and character of the weavers.

Ethnohistorian Malcolm Margolin's historical sketch is also in the catalogue. Margolin tells us that before the coming of the Europeans, the Pomos represented an "estimated 11,200 to 21,000 people" in what would become Mendocino, Sonoma, and Lake Counties...These diverse people, who did not in any way think of themselves as a single cultural or political entity, belonged to over seventy politically independent groups, village states they might be called..."

Margolin sketches Pomo history from before the collapse of the Mission system to the conquest of California by the United States. The record is an ugly one. Margolin writes:

> With the collapse of the Mission system in 1834, the southern parts of Pomo territory were given over to Mexican land-grant holders and the new overseers widely abused and even enslaved native people...

As for the United States, "...The history of the 1850s and 1860s is one of soul-sickening brutality, as native people were dispossessed, enslaved, hunted down and massacred in groups..." By 1910, writes Margolin, only 1200 survived.

As for recent history, despite "the last ten years' losses (there has been) something of a cultural renaissance as a younger generation has taken a new interest in the songs, dances, ceremonies, languages, and arts of their people..."

This book, then, is evidence of a people's talent and generosity. These weavers and basketmakers, women and some men, have broken with Pomo tradition in order to make sure the art continues. They have broken with tradition in order to keep tradition alive. They prove, as embodied in Else "Camache" Allen herself, that one can be proudly Native Californian without giving into hate. Mrs. Allen's desire to teach her people's art to non-Indians is a real act of faith.

News from Native California is a quarterly magazine of Native California life published by Malcolm Margolin that includes biography, articles, essays, and poems of Native California. The spring 1996 edition includes a sketch by Bev Ortiz, who also writes in *Remember Your Relations*. Her appreciative eulogy of Bun Lucas reminded me of Mrs. Allen and her life.

"During his life," Ortiz writes, "Bun found spiritual strength in both the Kashaya and Mormon religion. He told his stories in local schools. He became the first ever Coast Miwok to be hired as cultural interpreter." Ms. Ortiz writes of a brave, responsible man, an elder such as we would all be proud to have in our families. And that, I think, is the point—that men like Bun Lucas, women such as Elsie Allen, are extraordinary fellow Californians. They reached out to us, though their people had good reason to mistrust the stranger. These contemporary Californians were, as Mr. Lucas was named by channel 9's P.B.S., "local heroes." Their loss was a loss for all of us, not only for what they represented but for who they were. Their works and memories, at least in part, are still with us—thanks to the aforementioned writers and these publications, which have done so much to recover what might have been lost.

CHAPTER 17

Of Memory and Morality

Richard Rodriguez and Gary Soto

"I have become notorious among certain leaders of America's ethnic left. I am considered a dupe, an ass, the fool—Tom Brown, the brown Uncle Tom, interpreting the writing on the wall to a bunch of cigar smoking pharaohs...

"You who read this act of contrition should know that by writing I seek a kind of forgiveness—not yours. The forgiveness, rather, of those many persons whose absence from higher education permitted me to be classed a minority student. I wish they would read this. I doubt they ever will..."

—*Richard Rodriguez*, Hunger of Memory

An Argument for Richard Rodriguez

R ichard Rodriguez has been slandered by a radical academic community that has turned its back on the tenets of traditional liberalism. Like Shelby Steele, and in the giant footsteps of Ralph Ellison, Rodriguez is an ethnic writer who has addressed himself to American issues that are universal. He has used his ethnic background, both Spanish and Native American, to find links to a broader American community.

Rodriguez has been misunderstood, I believe, on three major issues—affirmative action, bilingual education, and cultural diversity and cultural pride.

While Rodriguez supports affirmative action, he does not support entitlements based solely on race. He opposes bilingual education, not because he is ashamed of his heritage—Rodriguez himself is bilingual— but because he believes that bilingual education keeps immigrant children from mastering English and becoming American citizens in the fullest public sense.

On issues related to cultural diversity, Rodriguez opposes the cheerleading that has become endemic to Women's, Ethnic, and Gay Studies. But, in his own writing, Rodriguez has honored the culture and life of his Mexican father.

Rodriguez expressed his feelings about affirmative action in a series of essays that pre-dated and were later included and revised for *Hunger of Memory*. In "None of This Is Fair" (anthologized in *The Complete Writer's Workout Book*, 1988, by D.C. Heath and Company), Rodriguez traces his concern about the misuse of affirmative action through an anecdote from his own life. Born in 1944, Rodriguez became a "scholarship boy" before the days of affirmative action. His road was difficult and the price paid for academic success was high. As a child of Mexican immigrants, the boy entered Sacramento's Catholic schools not knowing even 50 words of English. Spanish was the language of home, of family, of family protection, and love. When the teacher, a nun, asks Rodriguez's parents to speak only English at home, his parents comply. They are willing to sacrifice for their children's success, and Rodriguez owes his success, as he makes clear, to his mother and father, as well as the Irish teaching nuns and brothers and his liberal Protestant and Jewish university professors. Rodriguez's effort for his Ph.D. is due to his own hard work and to others' help as well. He is modest about his own accomplishments, but he also argues what we know in our hearts—that successful individuals have had many people help them on their way. Rodriguez has made the point, too (on National Public Radio), that his experience is not unique: we all depend upon help from those outside of our own ethnic and religious group—a fact that is very often unnoted and unnoticed.

"None of This is Fair" opens in 1974, when Rodriguez must choose where he will begin his teaching career. He wants no special privilege based on race. It is a point of honor. He is who he is, at great cost and pain and pride—to his parents and himself. He wants no racial entitlement.

As a Ph.D. candidate in Renaissance Literature, Rodriguez is besieged with job offers, even from universities where he has not applied, schools that seem to prize him not for his scholarship but for his surname. At one point, Rodriguez is challenged by a friend and colleague, a fellow T.A.:

> "It's just not right, Richard. None of this is fair. You've done some good work, but so have I. I'll bet our records are just about equal. But when we look for jobs this year, it's a different story... You're a Chicano and I am a Jew. That's the only real difference between us..."

Already ambivalent about affirmative action entitlement, Rodriguez reconsiders his academic career. He decides to reject all offers—to stand alone—to make it or not make it as a writer.

It would be a mistake to read Rodriguez's argument as an argument against affirmative action. The essay does not conclude with his rejection of academia. The essay concludes with a meditation upon those in our society who have been truly excluded. Rodriguez's writing is both poetic and compassionate. He argues against our hypocrisy. How easy it is to give a racial entitlement, a quota! How difficult it would be to help the devastated among our people, who, writes Rodriguez, "...do not ever imagine themselves going to college... white, black, brown. Always poor. Silent..."

He continues:

> ...the debate drones on and surrounds them in stillness. They are distant, faraway figures like boys I have seen peering down from freeway overpasses in some other part of town...

Bilingual education may have started with noble motives, but it is Rodriguez's belief, and not his alone, that bilingual education has been a failure. Rodriguez knows what his family sacrificed by giving up Spanish; he knows, too, what he and his brothers and sisters gained through mastery of English—full entry into American society. He writes in "A Bilingual Childhood" *(The American Scholar,* Winter 1980, later revised for *Hunger of Memory)*:

> Without question, it would have pleased me to have heard my teachers address me in Spanish when I entered the classroom. I would have felt less afraid. I would have imagined my instructors were somehow related to me. But I would have delayed—postponed for how long?— having to learn the language of public society. I would have evaded—and for how long?—learning the great lesson of school; that I had a public identity...

I do not know whether Rodriguez is wrong or right, or wrong and right, about bilingual education. Unlike many of his detractors, Rodriguez is himself bilingual, fluent in both English and Spanish. I do know that Rodriguez's arguments call for honest debate—not angry dismissal.

The last charge against Rodriguez—that he has turned his back on his culture and his family—I cannot understand at all. Both *Hunger of Memory* and *An Argument with my Mexican Father* are absorbed with the relationship of Rodriguez and his mother and father. The author's parents are described with affection, sadness, love, and respect. The distance that Rodriguez records—between immigrant parents and first generation American children—has been written about by writers as culturally diverse as Alfred Kazin, Irving Howe, Amy Tan, Jean Wakatsuki Houston, Jose Villareal, and William Saroyan. Like those other writers, Rodriguez does not celebrate distance but mourns it. That he accepts responsibility for the loss of intimate family love is an act of honesty, not of betrayal. In *An Argument with my Mexican Father,* Rodriguez pays homage to his father's moral strength and dignity. He believes that is what his father stands for—the way of Old Mexico, a way of bravery and dignity when facing life and death—is what we in California need now, at this time:

> ...his smile was loving. But his smile claimed knowledge. My father knew what most of the world knows by

now—that tragedy wins—that talent is mockery. In the face of such knowledge, my father was mild and manly. If there is trouble you want my father around...for my father is holding up the world, such as it is.

At Chabot College, during the past five years of instructing night classes, I have taught, at least ten times, "None of This Is Fair" to classes that included working-class Hayward Blacks and Latinos, as well as Mexican-Americans from the Fruitvale-East Oakland barrio. Many have not agreed with Rodriguez's view of affirmative action. Most believe that racial entitlement is a fair remedy for past discrimination. But all expressed respect for Rodriguez as a writer and a man. Regarding bilingual education, I have yet to meet a student who has not told me how relieved he was to be finally in English-only classes. None of my students expressed the belief that Rodriguez's essay showed shame for his Mexican heritage.

Let me state this clearly: Rodriguez is not a conservative. He is for affirmative action based not on race, but upon economic deprivation. He is for, as those who watch *MacNeil/Lehrer* know, almost unlimited immigration. He believes immigrants are the heart and soul of California's future. He has become, himself, a student of Mexican culture and history.

Richard Rodriguez is an essayist in the American tradition of Frederick Douglass, Thoreau, and Emerson. His style is lyrical, distinctive, and intellectual. He makes use of private experience to make a social argument. Some people may believe that Rodriguez's arguments are in error (I believe they are not). But to dismiss his essays, so well-written, so deeply considered, so filled with personal struggle and pain, is to disgrace the idea of academia itself.

Gary Soto, Prose Painter

Gary Soto is an acclaimed writer, a critical and popular favorite. He is also a professor of Chicano studies at U.C. Berkeley. Unlike Rodriguez, Soto is a second-generation Californian. Unlike Rodriguez, Soto was not of the working middle class. His family was poor. Both writers, though, have much in common. They are both Catholic, compassionately if not ritually so; they are moral, and through writing, they have found their place in the world.

Soto considers himself an essayist. He is, in fact, a superb short story writer, a prose painter of miniatures, in the great tradition of fellow Fresnan William Saroyan. Soto calls his work narrative recollections, but they are nonfiction short stories and they contain the poignancy of short fiction.

Soto suggests, in his pieces, contours of a whole life, and his sense of time is panoramic. I will focus, here, on three pieces. In the first, "This Man," Soto pays his respects to his late father and details permanent loss. In the second, "Being Stupid," Soto uses his experience to make a moral point about taking from others; in the last vignette, "Short Takes," Soto writes about his wife and daughter and exemplifies that love and continuity are our greatest treasures.

Soto begins "This Man" (from *Lesser Evils*):

> My father died in an accident and it was not accident that the man who fell on him and broke my father's neck never again came to our house, though he was a friend of the family who lived only five houses away...

More than 30 years after this tragedy, Soto reflects upon his father and thinks of the man who accidentally killed him. Regret, loss, and anger are given voice: "...we lived poor because he died. We suffered quietly and hurt even today. Shouldn't this mean something to him?"

Soto concludes by speaking of his brother, Rick, and himself and the brothers' continued sense of separation and loss: "...When we meet for Thanksgiving, his knee, like mine, jumps up and down. It won't stop. When I ask, 'What's wrong?' he says with his arms folded behind his head, 'Nothing. Nothing at all.'"

"Being Stupid" is a vignette from *Living Up the Street*. (The entire autobiography was a favorite of my Sophomore Literature class last year and I recommend it highly.) It deals with right and wrong and makes a moral point without directly preaching. In "Being Stupid," Soto allows himself to join his friend, Scott, in stealing a television and stereo from Scott's sisters.

Soto, in the story, shows how hard it is to take from others if we have a conscience. Gary feels guilt: "Of all people we stole from a relative. A sister...I said a made-up prayer and assured God if I got out of this one I'd be good. No problems from me, ever..." The young men sneak back into Scott's sister's home and return the goods. They drive home "sweating but relieved."

Soto offers here the opposite of gangster boasting. Kids, reading Soto, can identify with the non-swaggerer, the basically gentle non-hoodlum, the decent person, not perfect, who eventually does the right thing.

Living Up the Street concludes with Gary, now an adult, living in Mexico City with Carolyn, his wife, and Mariko, his infant daughter. "Short Takes" is dedicated to Soto's wife, Carolyn. The boy who early lost his father, who grew up in the barrio, who fought with his brother, who struggled for recognition, has found love and marriage and fatherhood and has become, too, an artist, a painter of words. Soto writes to his wife about their child.

> ...At fourteen months she was only confused at why she hurt her ankles and elbows...I rocked her at the dining room table as you tried to sing, coo, and clap her into happiness...

> Soto concludes, "...I walked for a while giddy with life for you and Mariko...."

Gary Soto helps us, as adults, appreciate life. As adults, we know what our students cannot yet know. We know how much Soto has succeeded, for we understand how difficult it is to overcome loss, to break out of poverty, how hard it is to hold love, to sustain marriage, how important it is to be a living parent. Soto's words define a man we can trust and admire. Soto has written his life with simplicity and warmth and yet with awareness of the real terrors of existence. He has written with no attempt to present himself as other than himself.

Ethnic Literature that Transcends

We have lived through a time so Orwellian that Louis Farrakhan, a man who is openly—to the point of near Nazism—anti-Semitic, anti-Catholic, anti-white, a man who celebrated the murder of Malcolm X, was invited at large fees to speak at public universities, while compassionate, original thinkers like Richard Rodriguez and Shelby Steele were ridiculed, called "Uncle Toms" and placed beyond the pale and off the required reading lists.

Ethnic literature should be large enough to include Shelby Steele and Alice Walker, Martin Luther King and Malcolm X, Amy Tan and Jean Wakatsuki Houston, Bernard Malamud and Saul Bellow, Richard Rodriguez and Gary Soto. Whether from the right wing or the left, propagandizing students is wrong. Real writers like Rodriguez and Soto both define and transcend their ethnicity. Soto and Rodriguez, here in California, have fulfilled Ralph Ellison's desire for American literature:

> the role of the writer is to...allow a universal identification, while at the same time not violating the specificity of the particular experience and particular characters...

We need both Rodriguez's honest arguments and Soto's hopeful true stories. Both men, all differences recognized, have enriched California literature and California life.

CHAPTER 18

San Francisco in the 1980s

Dorothy Bryant and Herb Gold

Two important Bay Area novelists, Dorothy Bryant and Herbert Gold, took on the assumptions beneath the surface of San Francisco during the 1980s. Bryant and Gold did not fall prey to the intellectual fashion of that time. Instead, they had the strength to oppose the prevailing wisdom that sexual expression somehow equaled, in and by itself, a social advance.

Bryant, no homophobe, had the courage in her book *A Day in San Francisco* to depict the sexual promiscuity of the 1980s Castro District not as a harbinger of freedom but as a symptom of illness. Her novel, which met with so much anger from homosexuals at its publication, has become tragic prophecy.

Gold's *A Girl of Forty* offers a look at the hedonists, men and women who live on the City's other side; his novel argues that sex can be used to create distance as easily as intimacy, and his novel ends, as does Bryant's, on a note of deep loss.

Both authors understand the consequences of our sexuality. Both stand for the idea that our sexual relationships—if they are serious—cannot be casual. Their San Francisco of the 1980s is a city of the lost, both on the streets and in the neighborhoods, people talking to themselves (many with good reason), men and women in view of skyscrapers and bridges who must make choices that either affirm or evade their humanity. Both authors make clear that the pursuit of sexual pleasure must be subordinated to the responsibility we owe one another as fellow humans.

Dorothy Bryant: *A Day in San Francisco*

During Gay Freedom Day 1992, Richard Rodriguez spoke on the *Mac-Neil/Lehrer News Hour* and traced the movement of the Castro District away from what novelist John Rechy called a "City of Night" toward a daylight place of real community. AIDS has devastated the Castro and it was Rodriguez's thesis that a truly caring community has responded to the tragedy and that the district defines itself now through acts of compassion that transcend sexual orientation. This information would not make Dorothy Bryant unhappy. *A Day in San Francisco* is not a tract against homosexuality. It is, however, a strong critique of the Castro District as it existed in 1980, on the edge of the AIDS epidemic.

Bryant, whose other novels include the acclaimed *Miss Giardino* and *Madame Psyche,* uses a trio of characters in order to press her argument. To the extent her characters' speeches are powerful—and they are—the novel has the feel of a strong play.

The novel's heroine is Clara Lontana, a woman of 50 and a native San Franciscan who grew up in the Mission District during the 1930s and 40s, back when the district was a working class Irish and Italian Catholic neighborhood. Bryant's San Francisco is the opposite of Saroyanesque; here, neighborhood is a trap, signifying mediocrity and repressed emotion. It was Clara's divorce and move to Berkeley with her young son during the early 1960s, the novel makes clear, that freed her to become a writer, a feminist, and a professor.

Bryant uses the device of quoting within the novel from one of Clara's published essays, an essay which tries to make plausible, through a discussion of Dan White, the idea that San Francisco is an oppressive city, historically run by an "old boys' network." The strategy of quoting from the essay helps establish the main character's viewpoint and prepares us for her later criticism.

Bryant, through Clara, gives us a world that was once defined narrowly through machismo, sports, and unthinking conformity to religious dogma in order to prepare us for her equally strong denunciation of a male homosexual ghetto, which is defined just as narrowly by narcissism, attempts at eternal youth, and hatred of women. What both worlds have in common, Clara concludes, is an inability to accept responsibility for one's actions.

Dan White's murder of Mayor Moscone and Harvey Milk and his subsequent light sentence are seen as the logical results of the primitivism of a district and mind-set that Clara had to escape.

> ...Members of the jury wept openly for Dan White. He was one of theirs, a martyr to old San Francisco, to things as they had been. I heard of the verdict from 200 miles away. My son, I am glad to say, was four times that distance...

The main character, then, and through her, the author, identifies herself as a supporter of homosexual rights.

The setting of the novel is Gay Freedom Day 1980, and Clara is in San Francisco to celebrate the day with her son, Frank, 30 years old and openly gay. She is back in her old neighborhood, sympathetic to her son and to the movement to which he belongs, until the events of the day lead her toward anger and censure. Through Clara, the reader experiences the dark side of gay life. Frank has hepatitis, the last in a long line of sexually transmitted diseases; he has had syphilis twice; he sees acting out sexually as a badge of pride. Clara's friend Arthur, a middle-aged music teacher who is homosexual and lives outside the Castro District, tells Clara that she is naïve in her understanding of the actuality and extent of her son's and others' promiscuity. Arthur's lover has died of Carposi's Sarcoma. Arthur asks Clara, "How promiscuous is Frank, do you know? Does he cruise baths, bars, toilets?" He continues, talking about his former lover, "Larry once boasted he'd had twenty-three contacts in one weekend." Yet, Arthur tells Clara, Larry died alone—with only Arthur to visit him in the hospital.

Clara enters the Castro Theatre, where as a girl she first heard about the bombing of Pearl Harbor, and views the act of a female impersonator performing a vicious parody of women. Clara and the lesbians present are outraged, but the male homosexual audience is delighted. Clara later confronts Frank with both her anger over the performance and her concerns over his own promiscuity, but she is dismissed by her son as being "just like any homophobe." The novel concludes with Clara, broken, talking to herself on the street.

A Day in San Francisco portrays homosexuals as more than victims; it sees both homosexuals and heterosexuals as humans who have the choice to be defined by more than sexuality. By the novel's end Bryant's attitude is clear; old San Francisco has indicted itself through the light sentence and sympathy given to murderer Dan White; gay male San Francisco, too, has indicted itself—through a flight from the responsibility sexually active adults owe to themselves and their partners.

Bryant's description, frozen now in time, was an attempt to arouse discussion about basic issues confronting San Francisco life.

By the '90s, the City has seemed to change. In response to the AIDS epidemic, straight San Francisco, also terrified of the disease, has become more openly tolerant to homosexual rights. And—in response to the suffering and death around them—homosexuals have become more responsible with their sexuality. Bryant's novel, written when it was, published when it was, stands as a courageous act. She asked the questions other straight supporters of gay rights were afraid to ask.

Herbert Gold: *A Girl of 40*

> "... In California we learn just like other people that life stops and life goes on: people get sick and people die; people fall in love, wear love out.... For those things it's just like any place in the world...."
>
> —*Herb Gold*, A Girl of 40

A Girl of 40 is the story of a party girl, her son, and one of her men, a U.C. Berkeley journalism teacher who is also the novel's narrator. The novel is set on the eve of the Reagan presidency and concludes during the height of the Reagan era in the mid-1980s. It powerfully documents the mood of that particularly decadent time. Characters—

seemingly cardboard at first—deepen as Gold documents the effect of his heroine Suki and her behavior upon her teenage son. Like Bryant, Gold does not paint a soft picture.

Each of his characters pays, and pays an enormous price, for his or her weakness and life of narcissism and emotional deprivation. Gold cannot see sexual relationships as inconsequential. And he takes on the post-hippie, part-hippie, part-Yuppie, New Age, wealthy bohemia with a vengeance. One enters in this novel a world of shallowness and pretense.

Suki is living out her, and her friends', particular version of the California dream. She has money, men at her beck and call, beauty, and an appreciation of the brilliance of her particular piece of San Francisco landscape. She does not have, until it is too late, an appreciation of how her actions hurt others. She is fueled by her anger towards her former husband, who pays child support but has emotionally deserted their son, and by a simple belief in an eternal youth that cannot be. She wants everything—her beauty, her men—to remain in present tense, frozen; but her son, Peter, grows from age 12 to age 16, becoming less and less loving, more and more tormented.

The novel traces Peter's disintegration, his rage at his mother's emotional abandonment of him, his anger at her for flaunting her sexuality in front of him. We follow Peter's lies (he accuses Frank, the narrator, falsely of molestation); we are taken on a journey that can only end tragically. From Pacific Heights to the Tenderloin, Gold documents a particularly nightmarish California landscape.

At the novel's conclusion, tragedy brings hope that recognition can save Suki's soul. And her soul, Gold implies, is what has nearly been lost in her pursuit of eternal youth and power over men, her ignorance of her son's emotional needs.

Towards a New California Dream

Both novels draw strength because they were not attacks from the Reagan-Bush-Quayle-Buchanan right. Bryant and Gold are asking us to examine not only the hypocrisy of the conservatives who live in Orange County but to examine, also, other kinds of hypocrisy—closer to home.

They challenge the idea, held by the politically correct of both right and left, that saying you are loving and compassionate means you are loving and compassionate. Both are making simple statements about our responsibility to others.

In these books, Bryant and Gold oppose the California Dream fantasy of eternal youth, endless second chances, New Age solutions, and offer the more enduring California Dream of human relations built upon tolerance of and responsibility to one's neighbor. The last California dream, these authors make clear, has yet to be achieved.

PART V
1970s to Present Time

CHAPTER 19

An Appreciation

Wallace Stegner and Hisaye Yamamoto

California English-language-arts teachers will be pleased to find a new anthology of literature for middle-to-high-school readers that features multicultural and regional selections of fiction and nonfiction. *Where Coyotes Howl and Wind Blows Free*, edited by Alexandra R. and Gerald Haslam, contains the work of 32 authors; their backgrounds and ethnicities may be diverse, but they all share the experiences of the book's subtitle, *Growing Up in the West*. Included in the volume are Hisaye Yamamoto and Wallace Stegner, both of whom are worthy of the overused adjective "great."

Hisaye Yamamoto

The lesser-known Hisaye Yamamoto is a writer of indelible power. Her major stories, few as they are, are masterpieces. Before Amy Tan, Maxine Hong Kingston or Jean Wakatsuki Houston, Hisaye Yamamoto gave life and substance to Asian-Californian and specifically Japanese-American existence. Her *Seventeen Syllables*, a winner of the 1986 American Book Award for Life Achievement from the Before Columbus Foundation, is a book that deserves to stand on the shelf next to the important works of California literature. But it is not only a book for the library. It is a book that should be taken off the shelf and read.

Seventeen Syllables is one of Hisaye Yamamoto's greatest stories. It is a work grounded in Japanese-American life and is also a work about universal human triumphs and tragedies. The story revolves around a young Japanese-American woman, her husband, and her sensitive daughter. The young woman is a gifted haiku poet, but her husband is consumed with anger and jealousy about her writing and any part of her life that he cannot dominate or control.

This story was adapted into an excellent PBS screenplay. The screenplay does the story justice and is a good example of the kind of story—small scale, ethnic, and regional—that never would have been dramatized if not for public television. The KCET, L.A. production captures brilliantly the scenes painted in words by Yamamoto. We see pre-World War II California, the immigrant Japanese-American community, the rural California of heat and dust. We view the poetry of the land and of the seasons, and we see the desolation of almost unbearable loneliness. We read the story and we are enlarged. We view the teleplay and we return to the text.

Hisaye Yamamoto's stories in *Seventeen Syllables* span 50 years of living and take us from the Los Angeles of the 1930s to the relocation camps of the '40s to modern Los Angeles of the 1980s. *Seventeen Syllables* includes, among its fifteen stories, the devastating "Yoneko's Earthquake," which details the tragic consequences of a Japanese mother's love affair with the Filipino hired man, her abortion and her sorrow—as seen through the eyes of the daughter. Other stories deal with anti-Japanese discrimination and the experience of the relocation camps, but the collection also demonstrates touching examples of friendship between people of different races. In "Reading and Writing," the daughter of a Japanese immigrant teaches a "hillbilly," whose "forefathers had come before the Mayflower," to read English. The friendship described between the two women in "Reading and Writing" exemplifies Hisaye Yamamoto's very personal vision of America and California. She cannot be easily categorized. Her stories—the opposite of formula—touch us in places that can only be reached by the poets of the heart.

Wallace Stegner

Wallace Stegner, who died at the age of 84 in an auto accident, was one of the most powerful writers to come out of the American West. Biographer, novelist, essayist, short story writer, teacher, ecologist, Wallace Stegner's career and life exemplified the best qualities of our region—independence of mind, tolerance of others, toughness seasoned with compassion, appreciation of our natural resources, and the fierce desire to protect our landscape for future generations.

Stegner demonstrated excellence in many genres of writing. His biography of Bernard De Voto is a nonfiction classic. His novels, from the early *Joe Hill*, a psychological investigation of those drawn to revolutionary movements, to classics such as *Angle of Repose*, about men and women coping with old age, are a unique product of an original and independent mind. Stegner's novels make us think about ourselves and our society. His essays and short stories also bear the stamp of an individual not going along with prevailing fashion. I admire Stegner's appreciation of John Steinbeck in his essay dealing with "Flight," and Stegner's poetic tribute to Norman Maclean's *A River Runs Through It* is written with unforced feeling and without jealousy. He relates his life as a boy to Maclean's great novella, and we are left both moved and instructed. Stegner's personal essays dealing with his mother and father are examples of autobiographical art and contain a depth of feeling. Stegner is so plain-spoken that we too easily underestimate what a powerful artist he really was. He was a profound American, Western, and California writer.

Wallace Stegner's collection of essays, *Where the Bluebird Sings*, was his final published book. He is a brilliant essayist and his comments about our literature are always of interest. But the heart of the collection, for me, is in two essays, the introductory essay and "Letter, Much Too Late," a tribute from the author to his long-deceased mother.

In "Letter, Much Too Late" Stegner gives faith to his vision of the West that is his deepest desire, a statement of hope that is linked to his feeling for his mother's life and her goodness of heart. Stegner relates his feeling for his mother with his feeling for our region:

> "... All you can do is try," you used to tell me when I was scared of undertaking something. You got me to undertake many things I would not have dared undertake without your encouragement. You also thought me how to take defeat when it came and it was bound to

now and then. I can hear you laugh while you say it. Any moment now I will hear you singing....

Yet we live in a landscape, here in California, here in the West, which has been ravaged by unscrupulous developers who enrich themselves even as they destroy our natural ecology and beauty. Stegner contrasts his mother and father to show us, in miniature, the war of the West between what Stegner calls "boomers"—those that move from place to place exploiting the environment and its people—and the "stickers"— those that preserve nature and strive to create human communities. Stegner writes to his dead mother about his father:

> You believed in all the beauties and struggles and human associations of place; my father believed only in movement. You believed in a life of giving, he in a life of getting....

Stegner makes it clear that we have, like his father, been consumed with "getting" to the point of nearly destroying our environment. Yet he reiterates the basic faith he learned from the example of his mother's life. The emerging West, Stegner believed, will be the product not of the boomers but of the stickers, "not of those that pillage and run but those that settle and love the life they have made and the place they have made it in."

Stegner hopes that we in the West will "work out some sort of compromise between what must be done to earn a living and what must be done to restore health to the earth, air, and water ..." He could have no better legacy than for the West to become the place he moved us toward in his writing—a West of the "stickers" not the "boomers," a place where humans live in real community and a place where nature is cherished and protected.

CHAPTER 20

Haslam's Oildale, Our California

"... Now he lays before you the ways and speech and life of a few people grouped in a certain place—his own place and that is one book. In time he and his brethren will report to you the life and the people of the whole nation.... And when a thousand able novels have been written, there you will have the soul of the people, the life of the people, the speech of the people and not anywhere else can these be had...."

—*Mark Twain*

Gerald Haslam's novel *Masks* (Old Adobe Press, 1975) is a work that extends Twain's and John Steinbeck's line directly. It is one of the "thousand able novels" that report to us "the soul of the people, the life of the people, the speech of the people...." *Masks* is a California novel that explores the lives of the sons and daughters of the Dust Bowl, one generation after *The Grapes of Wrath*.

Haslam is the author of many short story collections, including *Okies, Snapshots*, and *That Constant Coyote*. He is the author, too, of collections of essays such as *Coming of Age in California, The Other California*, and *Voices of a Place*. Additionally, he is the most important editor and anthologist we have in our state. His anthology, *Many Californias*, joins *California Heartland*, the book Haslam edited with James Houston, as an essential work of California literature and California history. Haslam's literary essays, too, are both works of art and authentic glimpses of our present and our past. He is, I believe, one of the most important California voices since Steinbeck. And, like Steinbeck, he is receptive, in his fiction and non-fiction, to the voices of others around him.

Those of us who heard Haslam's keynote at last summer's Steinbeck festival in Salinas will remember the author's eloquent definition of regionalism, which to him—as it was to Twain—is the universal landscape. For Haslam has perceived that what America represents to the world, California represents to America. Here, in California, we have been granted another opportunity to be fully human. Failure of community, for Haslam as it was for Steinbeck, is nothing less than a failure of the human spirit itself. Haslam has been an honest voice, reporting failures with successes. *Masks* is a crucial contribution to California heartland literature, painting a world of both tragedy and hope.

Conflicts Behind the Masks

In *Masks*, Haslam traces both the courage and the cowardice of the children of the "Okies." The author, who grew up in the tough Central Valley town of Oildale, knew first-hand the world of the children and grandchildren of the dust bowl migrants. The argument that Steinbeck illuminated in *The Grapes of Wrath*—the dispute between Pentecostal fundamentalism and Biblical demands for justice and brotherhood—is played out in 1970s dust and smog and summer heat. Haslam offers a solution that is finally only individual, yet the decisions faced by the novel's central figure will find resonance in anyone who has tried to mediate between the demands of family and conscience.

The novel's central figure, Junior, is a professor, an intellectual, a son of migrants who is now uneasy both in the academic-political world of the early 1970s Bay Area and in the "Little Oklahoma" of Oildale, which has not changed enough since his youth.

Junior is home because his mother is dying. Soon he is caught within his sister and brother-in-law's world of fundamentalist Christianity and vicious racism. He is torn between love for his mother and distaste for his younger brother, who committed suicide and is regarded in the family (his photograph displayed next to a representative of Jesus) as a saint.

Haslam explores a universal theme relating to change; for the professor who had escaped Oildale 20 years before realizes in his heart that he has never escaped, that for 20 years he has not faced the central realities of his childhood world.

It is a cruel world that *Masks* depicts, a world far from the original dreams of Junior's mother, a woman who could have modeled for the brave migrant mothers photographed by Dorothea Lange. Now, a mother faces death amid a family argument. Junior's sister tries to bar Junior's friend, a Mexican-American doctor, from the family home, though the doctor wants to save the mother's life. She will not allow, Junior's sister says, a Mexican to enter the house. Junior's young brother, an addict and wife beater, is revered as a saint because of his deathbed conversion; and Maggie, Junior's brother's wife, is cursed as a whore though she is the most compassionate and bravest of all the novel's women characters. The "Okie" victims of prejudice now spend energy venting hatred against Blacks and Mexicans and Catholics and Jews in a demonstration of bigotry.

The novel's power relates to the opposition of sexual cruelty and sexual love. When Junior leaves with his brother's hated wife, Maggie, it is his recognition of his loneliness and need for the comfort of shared love, which is contrasted with the cruelty of sex based only on instinct, domination, and exploitation of weakness.

The love affair is not written about in an explicit manner, yet it is truly felt; the reader understands, because of what was not made explicit, the need of two suffering souls for one another.

Junior's homecoming strips away the masks of religion, of phony sainthood (Junior's brother was a pimp, not a savior) and of pretend-self. A strength of the novel is that Junior must face his own responsibility for what his brother became. His mother dead, Maggie beside him, Junior can finally say goodbye to his childhood place and time, aware that his hometown will never leave him. *Masks* is realistic and nearly tragic and offers only the hope of a happy ending.

Haslam's prose has been compared to country music. The comparison makes sense because Haslam's tone, the conversations of his characters, the words said and the words left unsaid, all lend his writing a lyric power.

The novel is not Haslam's first or last word on the Okies. In later prose works, he has documented the movement of the children and grandchildren of the migrants into the middle class, into colleges, and work, and marriages and attitudes that would be anathema to the minor characters of *Masks*.

"Oildale"

Haslam's 1986 essay "Oildale" *(Voices of a Place)* should be read as a companion piece to *Masks*. Part of Haslam's unique biography is rendered in "Oildale"—an essay that fully integrates the individual and his family.

Haslam was born to an Anglo, Texas-born father and California-born Hispanic mother; he was both an insider and outsider in his hometown. A football player and an athlete, Haslam discovered books in high school, significantly *The Grapes of Wrath*. In Protestant Oildale, he attended Garces High School, a Roman Catholic Christian Brothers school. And later, in college and graduate school, Haslam's dedication to Central Valley experiences was met with scorn. "Who cares what happens in the sticks?" Haslam quotes one professor, commenting on the author's thesis. Haslam's nonfiction often celebrates his parents (his father, an All-American football player, was a man of physical and moral courage) and Oildale is, in part, a tribute to Haslam's mother and father, who rejected bigotry and racial prejudice.

> ... My own parents for reasons I've never fully understood—his better education, probably, and her Latin attitudes ... did not indulge in such delusion. Instead, they taught me to accept people as individuals....

As the author walks out onto the streets of his hometown, in December 1985 cold and fog, he understands how unusual his parents were and are; for bigotry in Oildale is still very much alive.

> ... And when things go wrong, as they so persistently do, someone must be blamed; mother dies and the damned

doctors are responsible, the car doesn't run and the dirty Japanese are guilty.... Niggers cause this and Jews and slopes but mostly niggers because blaming blacks has long been an acceptable way for lower class whites to vent general grievances....

Yet Haslam perceives that much of Oildale is not racist, that the children and grandchildren of the Dust Bowl and migrant camps have struggled and succeeded in California without wishing to inflict pain on others. He observes, "Oildale is not a breeding ground for fascism but poverty certainly is ...," and later in the same essay writes with pride:

> What fearers of fascism forget is that most of Oildale is populated by folks who have established themselves in the middle class by dint of hard work, whose daughters now aim for the honor roll and whose sons play football and fight wars....

Historian, anthologist, fiction writer, essayist—Haslam is a teacher. He instructs us that, unmasked, we have much in common. And following the L.A. riots, who can doubt we have been unmasked? All of us—African, European, Asian, Hispanic, and Native American—now have our innocent dead. Haslam's work, which should be taught in our high schools, bridges our various cultures, and moves us toward universal understanding. Haslam's work transcends racial boundaries.

In "Oildale" the author passes a church:

> I hear voices raised to a God, praying for me, their brother, burdened by sins unknown to them, but burdened, surely burdened, because that is the human condition and with God's help it can be endured....

By enduring, Haslam shows us, we open ourselves to the possibility of fellowship and love. Our future in California depends upon those values of morality, tolerance, and compassion for the helpless—all of which Haslam has detailed with quiet strength and honest feeling. Gerald Haslam, as writer and anthologist, is in the line of John Muir, John Steinbeck, William Saroyan, Theodora Kroeber, and Wallace Stegner. His work is an attempt to keep faith in a vision we must not let die. Haslam, in his own writing and as an editor, has respected the diversity of humanity within our region. Amid a decade of "multiculturalists" who have mainly reaped division—and right-wing ideologues who have exploited those divisions—Haslam stands in sharp contrast. The women and men he has written about and anthologized represent different races, ethnicities, religions, and economic classes—but they share a common humanity. Haslam's interest has been to help our students—and ourselves—perceive what unites us in California as humans in our suffering and in our triumphs. It is no small contribution in this age, at this time.

CHAPTER 21

Gerald Haslam's Human Truths

Straight White Male, Manuel and the Madman, and
Coming of Age in California

Gerald Haslam is the essential California Central Valley writer. Having grown up in the tough town of Oildale among children of the Dust Bowl migration, Haslam worked in the fields and packing sheds beside Latinos, Asians, and blacks.

Like Steinbeck's Okies, they had come to the Central Valley not in search of El Dorado, but to follow the more modest dream of a better life for themselves and their children. In his 30-year career, Haslam has paid tribute to this home place and written with empathy about its people, all without sentimentalizing the meaner aspects of valley life. In three recently published books, Haslam maintains that focus.

Straight White Male, Manuel and the Madman, and *Coming of Age in California: Personal Essays* are moral statements about our obligation to others. Without imitating the great Central Valley writers Steinbeck and Saroyan, Haslam extends their thinking, helping us understand how in this new century of innovative technology and affluent lifestyles the old human truths remain.

Straight White Male

Straight White Male is a novel that rebuts glib New Age psycho-babble about the aging and the aged, jealousy in marriage and raising teenage children. The narrator, Bakersfield-born Leroy Upton, is a successful man who is tested in middle age by the rebellion of his teenage son, by his anger about his wife's past and by the mental and physical deterioration of his elderly parents. Writes Haslam of a nursing home's residents:

At the nurse's station...twenty or so people in wheel-chairs, folks who cannot help themselves, being assembled like a wagon train fearing attack.

Upton's anxiety is that of a troubled, flawed man trying to do good by a devastated father, a bitter mother, a troubled son, and a loving but overburdened wife. He's honest enough to realize that all the clichés about the elderly are simply abstractions when dealing with the needs and pain of his parents. He knows there is no easy answer to this ordeal, that every choice will bring hurt and sorrow. Yet he learns that a caretaker's experience is more than guilt or resentment. Helping his parents leads him toward the reality of his wife's devotion and his son's sympathetic character.

In a series of well-conceived flashbacks, Upton, who lives in Mill Valley, California, recalls his growing up in the Bakersfield of the 1940s and '50s, and begins to understand that his working-class parents helped him create a life they could barely imagine themselves. In contrast to the novel's title, Upton ironically is much more than a stereotype of a "straight white male," and, along with the story's Bay Area and Central Valley characters, transcends the obvious trappings of gender, class, sexual orientation and race.

Manuel and the Madman

Likewise, Haslam's young-adult novel *Manuel and the Madman*, written with his wife Janice, takes us beyond simple-minded ideas about race. The novel details the evil of white racism, but also the hypocrisy of reverse discrimination.

Manuel Ryan is (like Haslam) of Anglo and Latino heritage. As a boy, after going to live with his grandmother when his parents separate, Manuel is befriended by a grandfatherly, Saroyanesque neighbor, Mr. Samuelian.

"[T]hese old narrow terms make no sense," Mr. Samu-elian says of how our society currently defines race. "...We are a blended people culturally and physically.

This blend, Haslam argues, is our great strength. For Haslam, American and Californian culture is a braided one, and needs to be accepted as such.

Coming of Age in California

We are all connected more than we know, even in our personal tragedies. This is what Haslam addresses in his nonfiction masterpiece, *Coming of Age in California*. One of the essays, "A Personal Cancer," is especially emblematic.

Here, Haslam describes his continuing battle with prostate cancer and links his suffering with that of others, including the 40,000 American men killed by the disease each year. He knows that for his wife and five grown children, "this is a family disease." When he learned of his diagnosis, "I stopped by St. James, lit a candle and prayed for the strength to deal with whatever I had to face."

We have an obligation, Haslam implies, to be just to others. We are obligated, he reminds us, not to live for ourselves alone.

CHAPTER 22

Pride of Place

Haslam's Valley

"In my heart, in the deepest part of me where I really live, I remain very much a product of my family and my region.... I found that the Great Valley grasped my innards like tree roots wrapping around and through so that it is difficult for me to tell if one exists independent of the other."

—*Gerald Haslam*

"People are places."

—*William Saroyan*

Many of my students are first-generation Americans. Their parents are from China and India, from Pakistan and Afghanistan, from Russia and Korea and Vietnam.

They are now Californians, children of the Bay Area, whose earliest memories are of Fremont. Their ancestral roots are both thousands of miles away and embodied through their parents in a specific California place. Immigrants and first-generation Americans now define Fremont as much as Saroyan's Armenian immigrants defined Fresno, as much as Gerald Haslam's Texas- and Oklahoma-born neighbors defined the Oildale and Bakersfield of the Great Depression and World War II era.

The power of regionalism in a literature is that the writer's immersion in a specific time and place and people allows the reader to find meaning in his or her own locality. If the regional writing has depth, the reader will find essential meanings in his or her own surroundings.

Gerald Haslam is a major regional writer in the tradition of Steinbeck and Saroyan. Yet Haslam is in the line not only of those California giants but also of other regionalists—Sherwood Anderson of *Winesburg, Ohio*, as well as William Faulkner, Eudora Welty, and Flannery O'Connor.

The book *Haslam's Valley* collects nearly forty years of quality writing set in Haslam's terrain, the Oildale of Okies, Mexicans, Blacks, and Asians who work hard for a living and struggle for respect and dignity. As always, Haslam illustrates that to write with love of one's region is not to be uncritical.

Powerful regional artists like Haslam are not cheerleaders. They look at their home place and can see, in that place, the cowardice as well as the courage of a whole world.

When Haslam exposes prejudice, as in a powerful early story called "The Doll," it would be a mistake to think that he is pointing a finger only at Central Valley bigotry. For Haslam's writing, which is in the tradition of Mark Twain, punctures human hypocrisy wherever it is found—and hypocrisy is, of course, found everywhere.

"The Doll" is about all of the comfortable and self-righteous who are insensitive to the suffering of others. In the story, two Oklahoma migrants, a boy and his mentally retarded uncle (who is as small and as delicate as a "doll") look for work. They offer to do chores for an Oildale matron of the comfortable middle class. The Oildale summer is sketched flawlessly, and we are immersed in the intense summer heat, while we hear the voice of the needy migrants and hear also the thoughts of the respectable Mrs. Hollis, who cannot understand what is in front of her eyes.

Haslam writes:

> The day was oppressively hot, even in the shade of the porch, but the Okies stopped in full sunlight on the front lawn. The larger boy, lean with dirty-looking yellow hair that contrasted with his deeply un-browned skin, answered in a flat, nasal voice: "Lookin' fer work, lady. Kin we mow yer law of anythang?"

He continues:

> Although her lawn was indeed shaggy, she didn't want this
> drippy-nose Okie near her any longer than necessary....

When she relents and hires the pair, she refuses to let the boy and
his uncle use her bathroom. When the uncle can no longer hold his
urine and "pisses hisself," the woman, who ironically considers herself to
be religious, shows no humanity or compassion.

Haslam's ending is devastating because he bases his short stories on
character, and thus allows the readers to draw their own conclusion as,
in this story, Mrs. Hollis comes to hers: "'Jesus didn't mean *them*,' raced
through her mind. 'He didn't. He wouldn't. He didn't.'"

Mrs. Hollis may call herself a Christian but she does not understand Christianity. And thus Haslam's exposure of hypocrisy could not
be more exact.

Writing in the years after *The Grapes of Wrath*, Haslam refuses to
see the "Okies" as mere stereotypes. Of Anglo and Latino background,
and a Roman Catholic, Haslam is very aware of the prejudices of his
hometown—against blacks and Asians as well as Mexicans, Jews, and
Catholics. He also is aware of working-class whites who belie the easy
categorizing of too many educated people who talk about "Okies" in a
dismissive way they would never employ when talking about African-
Americans or Asians or Hispanics.

In "The Great X-Mas Controversy," a drinker at the Tejon Club
discovers a Hmong family living as his own family once had—in tents
and in poverty. He realizes that the Hmong father, in his dignity and
desperation, is only looking to find work in order to feed his hungry wife
and children.

The narrator of the story, thinking of his own past, grows articulate.
The vernacular, recorded at perfect pitch, exposes great depth of understanding and an empathy that is both understated and totally sincere.

> They also looked real familiar. Whenever my folks come
> out here from Oklahoma, and I wasn't but a little kid,

we'd camped right here in these same woods. We'd built a shelter outta whatever we could find, just like these folks done, and me and my brothers and sisters we was hungry a lot, just like these kids. I have to tell you, it grabbed me damn deep to see folks livin' like that in California in the 1990s. And me with a well-fed family, two cars, two TVs, a nice house, a good job. It got me to thinkin'.

J. B., the narrator, organizes the men at the bar and their wives to help the migrant family with food and offerings of friendship.

Well, I felt funny, like my throat has went soft and my eyes were warm. But to tell you the truth, I was semi-proud of myself.

Other stories in *Haslam's Valley* include much-anthologized classics. One such piece is "Mal de Ojo," about an Armenian poet and his Wild-man "one-eyed" brother, and a half-Mexican, half-Anglo boy and his suspicious grandmother. The story is both a nod to Saroyan and a literary slice of California that is entirely Haslam's own. For Haslam, one of so many Californians who are both Anglo and Hispanic, has not chosen one ethnicity at the expense of the other. He has embraced an identity that is inclusive and real for thousands of Californians.

The essays that conclude *Haslam's Valley* are especially meaning-ful. Haslam's tribute to his mother and father and his wife, Jan, are a reminder of Saroyan's statement that "people are places." In Oildale, Haslam grew up with a mother who read to him and who encouraged him to explore the realm of literature. Just as important, Haslam's father, a former All-American football player, taught the potential author to never give up, on the playing field or in life.

Now over 70 years old, a grandfather many times over, Haslam writes of his father Speck, and his suffering at the end of his life. "A rabbi once observed, 'Not to know suffering means not to be a man,'" Haslam continues, regarding his father: "Afflictions purged him of many things but not of tenacity or valor...." Haslam, too, who with his wife took care of his parents in their final years and illnesses—and who himself has battled prostate cancer—is a brave man. He is also a courageous literary artist who decided early in his career to write, come hell or high water, about what he named the "Other California."

He has been true to his place and his people: "As a result, my stories are about individual characters who are not generalizations. I want those creations to be faithful to their times and places and to the human condition, and to be distinct. If that is accomplished, I'm satisfied."

Someday writing students in places all over California and the West will no longer be talented beginners. In five or ten or fifteen years, they will write of their place and our regions. Out of their published stories and essays and poems, readers will encounter a region on the map that, like *Haslam's Valley*, will also be a place of the human heart.

Valley Memories

Richard Dokey

During a gray cold valley winter day in 1970 in Sacramento State College in the library, I found the short story "Sanchez" by Richard Dokey in a back issue of *The Southwest Review*. I felt the surge of pride you feel at the success of someone you know, in this case my high school creative writing teacher.

It had been more than a year since I'd been a student of Dokey's at Lincoln High School, a year that seemed, now that I was in college, to have taken place an eternity before. Yet Dokey's lessons were vivid to me. He had taught us to see as a writer sees—to look at life with an eye towards capturing a moment in time. He spoke to us of how he, as a writer, viewed skid row Stockton—how he noted the look of the facade of an old brick hotel, or stopped to observe the way a Filipino fieldworker held his cigarette, or listened to the way rain sounded on a downtown street in spring.

Richard Dokey saw Stockton with a poet's eyes, and he imparted some of that poetry to us. He told us to write of our own experience. He taught Hemingway and Steinbeck from a writer's point of view. We saw, because of him, writers as people who created out of the same emotions we experienced. His criticism was constructive and precise.

Today Dokey's writing is recognized. His story "Sanchez" has been anthologized a dozen times (it currently can be found in *California Heartland*, Capra Press). Gary Soto, James Houston, Gerald Haslam— all have included his work with the best of California and West Coast writing. Dokey's nonfiction narration "Going in Naked" can be found in *California Childhood*[1], and his major collection of short stories, *August Heat*, is available from Story Press[2]. Another excellent short story collection, entitled *Sundown*, is available through Seven Buffaloes Press[3].

What I best remember, though, and appreciate are Dokey's qualities as a teacher. He did for us what I try to do for my writing students now, which is to help high school seniors slow down, observe, trust their best instincts, and so catch the beauty and poignance and poetry of themselves alive upon an earth moving quickly through time. Even now I can still picture myself and my baseball teammate and childhood friend Tom Gulick walking home on a March afternoon of our senior year following Dokey's class. We lit cigarettes and we smoked under the long, overcast sky and we could smell the coming rain. We were not boys and not yet men, though Tom would be married before he was 20, and his son now is older than we were then. We walked past the tall valley oaks, graceful with dark, haunted branches. Instead of talking about baseball, Tom and I spoke about the writers we admired and the places they had described. We spoke of Steinbeck's Salinas and Monterey, of Mark Twain's Mississippi River, of Hemingway's Michigan, of Kerouac's Lowell. We wanted to see the places we'd read about. And we spoke of our childhood—now passing—and we felt the truth of what William Saroyan once called "the warm quiet valley of home." We walked between the Coast Range and the Sierra and looked west to Mt. Diablo, the mountain that overlooked our youth. We longed to leave the valley forever and never look back, and at the same time, we wanted to never leave Stockton, never to leave home.

We felt the poetry that our teacher, Richard Dokey, never called poetry. And we felt, too, encouraged by our teacher, that in writing we might capture what otherwise might be forever lost.

---

[1] Creative Arts Book Company, 833 Bancroft Way, Berkeley, CA.
[2] P.O. Box 10040, Chicago, IL 60610.
[3] Box 249, Big Timber, Montana.

About The Author

Marek Breiger grew up in Stockton, California in the San Joaquin Valley. He holds a B.A. in English and an M.A. in English, with a concentration in Creative Writing from San Francisco State University. He has long been an advocate for California literature and its importance as a way of understanding California history and life. He has published over 40 essays dealing with California literature and life in various books, magazines, and newspapers, including the *San Francisco Chronicle*, the *Daily Review*, *Inside English*, *Redwood Coast Review*, and *Western American Literature*, and the anthologies *Where Coyotes Howl and Wind Blows Free* (University of Nevada Press); *Updating the Literary West* (Texas Christian University); and *Oakland Out Loud: The Oakland PEN Anthology*.

Breiger served for five years as a Resource Person at Asilomar for groups dealing with "Universal themes in California literature." He has twice won Dorothy Wright Awards from San Jose State University for "promoting love of literature and writing," as selected by San Jose State University English majors.

Breiger has taught high-school English for 33 years, at both the high school as well as community college levels—specifically, Berkeley High School, Moreau Catholic High School, and Chabot Community College. Currently, he teaches Language and Composition as well as other literature classes at Irvington High School in Fremont. He has taught at Irvington since 2000.

He wrote two columns in *California English*. "California Classics and Contemporaries," dealing with California literature, appeared from 1992-1995. "Breiger's Bookshelf" appeared from 2000-2005.

Breiger is a member of Oakland PEN. His essay "Who We Are," dealing with immigrant life in California, will appear in the forthcoming *PEN Oakland* anthology.

CPSIA information can be obtained at www.ICGtesting.com
Printed in the USA
LVOW11s1743250216

476712LV00001B/133/P